CASTLE ON A HILL

O beautiful Kishwaukee, placid stream,
With the wildly rushing waters seen in dream!
On thy early shores the red men came and went,
By the alder trees and birches pitching tent;
Earnest of the might future yet unseen
By the fairy, purple flowers leaved in green.

CASTLE ON A HILL

Glen A. Gildemeister

THE
DONNING COMPANY
PUBLISHERS

DEDICATION

This book is dedicated to Sally Stevens. In her long career at NIU and now in retirement, Sally's integrity, enthusiasm, hard work, generosity, and dedication have shown all of us what it takes to turn a dream into reality. The castle on a hill of 1899 became the extraordinary university Northern is today through the work of people like Sally. From the whole Northern family, Sally, "Thank you."

The Donning Company Publishers
184 Business Park Drive, Suite 206
Virginia Beach, VA 23462

Steve Mull, General Manager
Barbara Buchanan, Office Manager
Pamela Koch, Editor
Lynn Parrott, Graphic Designer
Stephanie Bass, Imaging Artist
Mary Ellen Wheeler, Proofreader
Cindy Smith, Project Research Coordinator
Scott Rule, Director of Marketing
Stephanie Linneman, Marketing Coordinator

G. Bradley Martin, Project Director

Library of Congress Cataloging-in-Publication Data

Gildemeister, Glen A., 1945–
  Castle on a hill / Glen A. Gildemeister.
    p. cm.
  Includes index.
  ISBN 1-57864-312-0 (hard cover : alk. paper)
  1. Northern Illinois University--History. I. Title.
  LD2341.I565G55 2005
  378.773'28--dc22

                    2005012291

Printed in the United States of America at Walsworth Publishing Company

CONTENTS

FOREWORD

It is an odd fact of university life that institutions established for the express purpose of creating and sharing knowledge often fall short in attempts to present the rich complexity of their own histories. Trained as we are in the exactitude of our various disciplines, university history as presented by academics is often ponderous and dry—long on facts and figures, short on color.

Happily, none of those shortcomings interfere with the reader's enjoyment of the volume you now hold in your hands. *Castle on a Hill* does an admirable job of tracing the growth of a tiny teachers college into a major research institution—and it does so in a way that both informs and inspires. As presented in these pages, the story of Northern Illinois University unfolds in richly human terms, reminding readers of nothing so much as an afternoon spent poring over a family album.

To the mostly nameless photographers who captured a century's worth of images, to the hundreds of contributors who saved pieces of the historical record, and to the modern-day archivist who breathed life into this project, all who cherish NIU owe a debt of gratitude.

John G. Peters
President

ACKNOWLEDGMENTS

Four very skilled and dedicated photographers created the images for this pictorial history: Keith Lowman, Barry Stark, George Tarbay, and Scott Walstrom. It is their excellence you see on the following pages. For reading drafts, improving the text, and helping to remove errors, I am in debt to Norm Gilbert, Mike Korcek, Ging and Jerry Smith, Sally Stevens, and Jerry Zar. Don Brod worked with me long, long ago on the first draft. Brian Eberly, Joan Metzger, and Edie Watje checked facts in the book. Without the generous support of Dean Arthur P. Young, University Libraries, the book would not be in print. Thank you all.

"The Normal Girl" (from a lantern slide, 1899)

chapter one

FOUNDATIONS LAID

Every institution begins life as one person's vision for the future. In 1894, DeKalb newspaper editor Clinton R. Rosette created the vision of a Northern Illinois Normal School to train teachers for the northern region of the state. Rosette, a young and intrepid political activist, supported John Peter Altgeld's campaign for the Illinois governorship in 1892. Of the twelve newspapers' editors in DeKalb County, only Rosette proudly claimed membership in the Democratic Party camp. When Altgeld won, he offered Rosette a choice of political appointments. Rosette wanted to stay in DeKalb and asked to be appointed to the statewide Normal School Board. While gaining valuable political experience on the board, Rosette began to forward the idea for a school in the northern third of the state to complement schools in the central and southern regions of Illinois. Rosette had the support of one other prominent local Democrat, the publisher of his newspaper, Joseph F. Glidden.

Rosette's roots in education ran deep. He was born October 24, 1850, in Paw Paw Township to William C. and Elizabeth Rosette, one of ten children in the family. He attended the usual one-room country school and then East Paw Paw Academy where, once graduated, he joined the faculty. While teaching, he studied medicine part-time for five years but abandoned that dream when he married Alpha C. LeClair on Christmas Eve, 1873. The new couple moved to DeKalb where they opened a private school at the corner of Main and Second Streets. Within four years, enrollment reached 125, but already Rosette began to follow his other love in life, journalism, as editor of the DeKalb County Chronicle. Just four months after the paper published its first edition on March 8, 1879, the owners, D. W. Tyrell and Company, sold it to Joseph Glidden. The Glidden/Rosette partnership would prove to be critical fifteen years later in bringing the new normal school to DeKalb.

Joseph F. Glidden

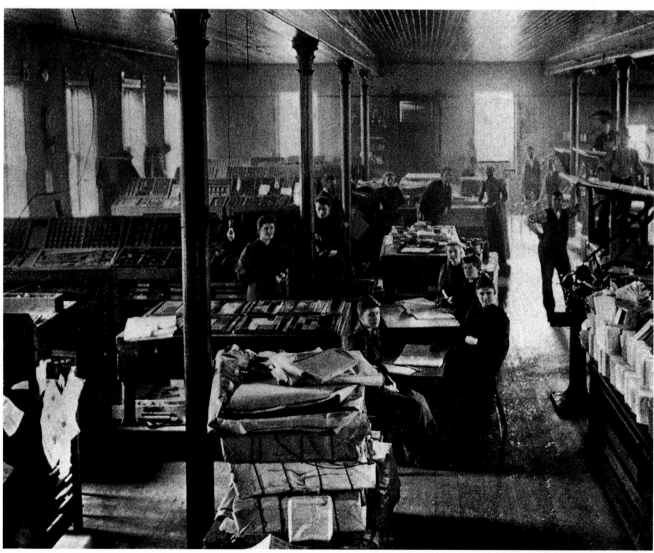

A one-term governor who accomplished much in his four years, John Peter Altgeld is best known for his pardon of the Chicago Haymarket anarchists, his support for higher education, and his partiality for Tudor Gothic architecture.

In 1895, the Illinois Legislature approved the creation of normal schools for the eastern and northern regions of the state, and communities began to lobby legislators to secure the new school for all the benefits it would bring. One of the frontrunners for the site of the northern normal school was Dixon, Illinois. However, the Legislature chose DeKalb in a competition with Dixon, Rockford, Polo, Oregon, Fulton, and Freeport. Dixon already had the privately owned Northern Illinois Normal School pictured here.

When Northern's first building opened, it became known as the "Castle on a Hill." It was just one of several Tudor Gothic buildings built on campuses during Altgeld's governorship. Known for decades simply as the Administration Building, Northern's trustees in 1964 named the building for John Peter Altgeld. Its complete rehabilitation became the centerpiece of the university's Centennial Celebration. The original structure took four years to build and cost $230,000; the remodeling took a bit longer and came in at $24 million.

J. B. Dille had established the Dixon NINS September 2, 1881. Dille proposed the school to the Lee County trustees promising to "maintain Classical, Scientific, Normal and Business courses for study and to have an attendance of 250 students, provided the citizens of Dixon would purchase and generate the payment of $25,000 to be redeemed in scholarships good in any department." For the first few years, Dille leased the abandoned Rock River Seminary Building that stood along the banks of the Rock River. He hired former associates and classmates from Valparaiso University in Indiana for staff and faculty. With enrollments surpassing hopes, Dille began construction on two new three-story buildings in 1882, one a women's dormitory. By the 1890s, over two thousand students enrolled in a wide range of courses including law, business, performing, and liberal arts. The opening of the new normal school in DeKalb, however, quickly cut the enrollments in Dixon and it officially closed in 1914.

In the competition for the location of the new state normal school, the administration in Dixon even offered to donate the site and buildings to the state if the new school were to be located in Dixon.

Rockford, Polo, Oregon, Freeport, and DeKalb provided competition for Dixon when the legislative committee began to look at sites, but it would take an extraordinary effort to secure the site. Even Dixon's generous offer would prove not to be enough. Clinton Rosette, editor of the DeKalb Chronicle and president of the Illinois Press Association, set to work to line up the needed support to bring the prize to his hometown.

Joseph Farwell Glidden, shown right posing for his ninetieth birthday portrait, was one of the three DeKalb patriarchs who would ally with Clinton Rosette to bring the normal school to DeKalb. Glidden owned the DeKalb Chronicle that Rosette edited and had built a local and national reputation for his invention of barbed wire in 1873. He was also a longtime political participant having been elected sheriff as a Democrat in 1852. A hardware merchant and local farmer, Glidden took an interest in many local ventures including the building of a large hotel in downtown DeKalb that bore his name. His primary contribution to the cooperative effort to lure the legislators to vote for DeKalb was the donation of sixty-three acres of his farm for the campus along the Kishwaukee River just west of downtown.

Longevity is a hallmark of the Glidden family: Joseph died peacefully on October 9, 1906, at the age of ninety-three. Annie Glidden, his niece, lived to see one hundred years, and his grandnephew, Charles Bradt, celebrated his one-hundred-and-first birthday in 2004.

Northern students for years have purchased flowers for special occasions at Glidden Florist next to the family homestead. The Glidden Heritage Association is working to preserve the barn in which "Uncle Joe" invented barbed wire. The homestead is now a museum commemorating this extraordinary DeKalb family. A large oil portrait of Joseph Glidden painted in 1899 by A. F. Brooks hangs in the main lobby of Founders Memorial Library. Glidden, along with Isaac Ellwood, Jacob Haish, and Clinton Rosette, are considered the founders of the university.

Built in 1876, the Glidden House Hotel on Main Street in downtown DeKalb became the headquarters for the new president of the Northern Illinois Normal School, John Williston Cook. When construction of the president's house fell behind schedule, Cook took rooms at the Glidden House in the summer of 1899 and held faculty meetings there until his house was ready in the spring of 1900. The hotel, gas-lit and steam-heated, offered about one hundred guest rooms, a formal dining room, and several convenience shops on the first floor, including a barbershop and bar. Rooms at the time rented for about two dollars a day or sixty dollars per month, about 20 percent of Cook's salary of $300 per month. Since Colonel Ellwood had promised to build the president a house, Cook may not have had to bear the cost of the rooms himself. The hotel remained a prominent fixture in downtown DeKalb until a fire destroyed it in 1962.

Jacob Haish was the second of the three barbed wire patriarchs. Born in Germany in 1827, Haish immigrated to the United States in 1835 and arrived in DeKalb in 1853. A hardware man, inventor, and longtime rival of Isaac Ellwood, Jacob Haish was also a major manufacturer of barbed wire. Haish fought an eighteen-year legal battle with Ellwood over patent rights that he finally lost in the U.S. Supreme Court in 1892. Haish donated $10,000 to build Northern's first gymnasium and the school library. The Haish Library remained the centerpiece of Altgeld Hall from 1899 until 1951 when the Swen Parson Library was completed. Haish died in 1926, just two weeks short of his ninety-ninth birthday. He, too, left an extraordinary legacy to DeKalb including an opera house, a hospital, a bank, and a public library, all of which bore his name.

With the fortune he amassed in the manufacture of barbed wire, Haish opened DeKalb's first large bank and anchored himself on Main Street just a block from the hotel Joseph Glidden had built years earlier. Local legend has it that Haish regularly sat just outside the front door to hold court on all issues of local import. The photo below of Barb City Bank dates to 1897.

Colonel Isaac Leonard Ellwood was the wealthiest and most influential of DeKalb's three patriarchs. In 1851, Ellwood, then just eighteen years old, set out to the California Gold Rush. After several years in the gold fields, he took a job at a hardware store in Sacramento. In 1855, he gathered his savings and headed east, stopping to see his brother Reuben in DeKalb. He sought a place to stay in Kingston on Henry Miller's horse farm and fell in love with the farmer's daughter, Harriet. He established a hardware store in DeKalb, married Harriet, and made a fortune in barbed wire. Colonel Ellwood also threw his considerable political weight behind DeKalb's bid for the new normal school and built a house for the first president, which he donated to the school.

The barbed wire manufacturer died September 11, 1910, at the age of seventy-seven and left an estate of nearly $30 million. The extraordinary mansion Ellwood built for his family remains today as a part of DeKalb's cultural heritage. Ellwood's creation is now part of the DeKalb City Park District, and the Ellwood House Association maintains the Victorian mansion as a museum. One of DeKalb's cultural jewels, the Ellwood House Museum has been featured in everything from tourism brochures to national television programs.

This 1894 photograph shows the main DeKalb barbed wire mills parallel to the railroad tracks just northeast of downtown. It was the invention and manufacture of barbed wire that brought fame and fortune to DeKalb in the last two decades of the nineteenth century. All three of the barbed wire patriarchs contributed to Rosette's effort to get a normal school for DeKalb.

Three things transformed the western two-thirds of the United States in the nineteenth century: the repeating rifle, the railroad, and barbed wire. Barbed wire fencing spread swiftly across the Trans-Mississippi West, marking the end of the open range in many places. The introduction of the new wire led in some cases to range wars with the cattlemen who fought to keep the open range. But sales boomed and the wire moved from the DeKalb wire mills and railhead all across the West.

On October 1, 1895, a crowd of around 30,000 people trekked to DeKalb for the groundbreaking ceremonies. The Sycamore City Weekly reported: "The lowest estimate placed on the crowd at DeKalb, Tuesday, when ceremony day was celebrated, was 20,000. Some say 35,000 were there. . . . The town can point with pride to the excellent manner the people were provided for both as regards comfort and entertainment. The weather could not have been better suited to the occasion. . . . There were tents, headquarters for various societies, the administration tent and others. Just west of these and at the edge of the timber, a stand and seats were erected for the evening concert. The concert was exceptionally fine, and the fireworks were better than before seen in the county." The derrick in this photo lifted the cornerstone into place, and Illinois Grand Master Mason Leroy A. Goddard began the ceremonies.

Altgeld Hall Cornerstone, 1895

Since there was only one building, the name of the school and the building were, at first, synonymous. A nickname, the "Castle on a Hill," soon took hold. When Williston Hall and other buildings became part of the campus, the Castle was known officially as the Administration Building until renamed Altgeld Hall in 1964. Architect Charles E. Brush, Chicago, designed and engineered the building; William J. McAlpine, Rochelle, was the general contractor. It took four years to complete construction at a cost of $230,160 and provided a total of 132,907 square feet for offices, classrooms, an auditorium, a gymnasium, a library, and boiler rooms.

The construction workers in the photo at the bottom enjoyed a shooting contest during their lunch break. They took advantage of the wide-open area to the northeast of the construction site that was the DeKalb Fairgrounds along the banks of the Kishwaukee River.

Altgeld Hall Construction, 1897

Once completed, locals quickly adopted the "Castle on a Hill" nickname. The medieval-looking figures that still adorn the battlements of Northern's first building are among its most distinctive features. The gargoyles are waterspouts designed to route water from the roof whereas the grotesques and griffins are merely decorative sculptures combining human and animal characteristics. Griffins, for example, combine the features of a lion and an eagle and may be found at the corners of the building striking a fearsome pose. Charles Brush placed eleven grotesques along the roof battlements and around the central tower of the original building. These sculpted figures served no function but brought a Gothic feel to the Castle and they became, over the years, the source for many campus stories and legends. To commemorate the university's centennial, Altgeld Hall has been completely restored outside and built anew inside at a cost of $24 million.

Altgeld
Hall
Grotesque

Dressed for
Easter, 1996

Gargoyle
Entwined in
the Ivy of
the Tower

Of the eleven original grotesques, only eight remained when the centennial restoration of Altgeld began. Lightning knocked one of the grotesques from the roof in the 1960s, but it was repaired and put into the small garden between Altgeld and Still Halls. Over the years, it became a common sight to see special decorations adorning it as students celebrated Halloween, Christmas, Valentine's Day, and commencement. These mystic sculptures have always attracted attention. Vandals severed the head from the torso in 2000, but concrete surgery managed to reattach the head with minimal scarring.

An informal contest held by the student newspaper in 1996 chose the name "Olivegoil" for the fallen grotesque, perpetuating the confusion between gargoyles and grotesques. In the top right image, art students had decked out the fallen grotesque for Easter.

Gargoyles, a means to drain water away from buildings, go all the way back to antiquity. Both the Egyptians and Greeks used animal-shaped hollowed sculptures to drain water away from large public structures. The idea expanded in the European Middle Ages when architects discovered that dividing the flow of water from the roof would minimize building damage. Sculptors of gargoyles operated under less restraint than other sculptors and used several animals and distortions in their creations. In a preliterate culture, they became symbols for both the church and the folk mysticism prevalent in the area as they commonly adorned castles and cathedrals alike.

The griffin is a mythological creature composed of the body of a lion and the head of a bird, usually an eagle. The Altgeld griffins feature the head of an owl. In an essay published in Northern's yearbook in 1909, student Laura Thompson suggested that the owl "shall symbolize our youth after they have been trained in our noble halls."

Workers set the seal, done in black and white mosaic tiles, into the main entryway. The original now may be seen in the entryway to Founders Memorial Library. Northern has changed its name three times since it opened in 1899 to Northern Illinois State Teachers College (1921), Northern Illinois State College (1955), and Northern Illinois University (1957).

Crimson Day Parade, September 23, 1899

Northern's grand opening took place from September 21 to 23, 1899, in a three-day festival called *Crimson Days*. Classes had begun on September 12. Like the huge celebration for the groundbreaking four years earlier, all of the communities surrounding DeKalb pitched in to make this a once-in-a-lifetime party. Once again, it was the local business people and politicians who took the lead in raising the necessary funds and organizing the many activities. The *Sycamore City Weekly* reported that the event "cost the city of DeKalb more than $6,000 to top the 1895 effort. The celebration was of much greater magnitude than ever before attempted in the county and was well managed." Civic decorations, parades, picnics, business exhibits, band music, and plenty of speeches provided activities from dawn to dusk each day. A taste of Chicago was part of the festivities with the Pullman Military Band playing, carnival acts performing, and a number of pickpockets working the large crowds. Heavy rains on Friday forced cancellation of Dedication Day and postponed the fireworks Saturday night.

Undaunted by the poor weather, these elegantly dressed women in the top photo simply added parasols to their outfits and continued marching in a rather bedraggled Friday parade.

The Normal School had no dormitory, and all students lived in town. Most walked to class up College Avenue and across the Kishwaukee River bridge. Kishwaukee is the English approximation for the Potawatomi word for cottonwood trees, and the river is one of the few in North America to run from south to north. It empties into the Rock River near Rockford.

College Avenue Bridge, 1899

Just behind the "No Shooting on Grounds" sign, the groundskeeper was lining the tennis court to prepare it for student use. The sign resulted from the noontime shooting matches commonly held by construction workers (see picture on page 9) on their lunch break. A prankster had put the stuffed owls on the sign and then later erased the "S" so the sign read "No Hooting on Grounds." The area being lined for a tennis court had been part of the DeKalb County Fairgrounds and would later be the home for Northern's football and track teams for over a half-century, Glidden Field. Today, a parking lot for the art and music buildings covers this spot.

First Athletic Facility, 1900

The main, formal entrance for the new normal school was on the south end of Castle Drive to DeKalb's Main Street. The lagoon created by damming the Kishwaukee River during the site competition visit soon became a permanent fixture of the grounds. Northern's trustees allocated $8,000 for landscaping the area in 1905, and laborers moved a total of 25,000 cubic yards of earth to enhance the lagoon and build garden terraces stretching down from the Castle to the lagoon and river. The student newspaper reported that "the old ice pond will be greatly enlarged, and the present water level raised about six feet. The shore line will be made irregular with gulfs, bays, peninsulas, and island features." Northern's first professional groundskeeper and gardener, Frank K. Balthis, came from the Shaw Botanical Gardens in St. Louis and put the finishing touches on the lagoon area. Balthis worked closely with biology and botany professor Fred Charles in choosing trees and plants for the grounds.

One of the centerpieces of the university's Centennial Celebration was the restoration of the Castle Drive gates and new landscaping to provide an attractive entrance to the old campus from Lincoln Highway. Dedication of the new gates marked the one hundredth anniversary of the founding of Northern on October 1, 1995.

One of the first campus landmarks, this fieldstone and mortar creation still stands one hundred years later as a place to sit, study, sleep, relax, or just reminisce about the good old days. It is located just off Castle Drive about halfway from the gates to Altgeld Hall and has introduced generations of new students to the pleasures of the lagoon.

Freshman Bench, 1900

In addition to the formal gardens built on the grounds, Professor Fred Charles and Frank Balthis combined talents to build Northern's first indoor botanical conservatory in 1906. A large structure built directly to the north of the main building, the Plant House functioned both as a teaching laboratory for botany students and a nursery for campus gardens. In 1908, Balthis noted with great pride that over 2,000 plants had been set successfully into the terraced gardens the previous summer, and work would continue to beautify the area surrounding the newly enlarged seven-acre lake. The next year, Balthis published a complete inventory of the total of 385 species and varieties represented in the Plant House that included the musa sapientum variety banana tree (photo at right). Given the harsh northern Illinois winters and the primitive state of insulation and heating at the time, the Plant House success was extraordinary.

While Frank Balthis built the Plant House, Professor Charles built a small zoo next to it. Betsy, a small black bear, joined the zoo in 1905. Here she is seen lapping from a mug held by Professor Charles who had slipped into President John Williston Cook's automobile for a photograph. Betsy, born in Wisconsin, came to DeKalb eight months old as a pet for Perry Ellwood, who then gave her to the Northern zoo. Domesticated by Professor Charles, Betsy was a big hit on her trips out into the DeKalb elementary schools. She died suddenly on December 20, 1906, just over a year old, with no hint of illness preceding her death. The student newspaper noted, "we should hesitate to intimate that Betsy was poisoned although several valuable dogs in DeKalb met death by that means the same week. There was evidence that she had been given something that did not agree with her." Charles took her carcass to a local taxidermist, and soon she was back in the biology lab for all to see: "Betsy is back. She is not as active as she once was, but the taxidermist has succeeded in making her look quite natural," the student newspaper reported.

Altgeld Hall Foyer, 1900

There were no dormitories or cafeterias, and most students brought a lunch to school each day. A group is seen at the top gathered inside the main entrance to the Castle getting a bit of reading and socializing done while having lunch.

The Northern Illinois, *in a story titled "The Mirror Line," described the scene: "You rush in, drop your books in some convenient unoccupied spot, and prepare to have just one look in the mirror before you go to class. But, alas for your hopes of even so much as a peek, for there you find a line of girls, mostly Juniors, gazing with rapt attention into the mirror above. They are evidently entranced by what they see for they can hardly tear themselves away. One girl, in particular, is arranging and rearranging her hair, first this way, then that, to see which style will increase her height the most. . . . You wonder if they'll ever get away from there when suddenly you are pushed aside and a curly-headed little Freshman trips gaily past you, utterly unconscious that she is taking your place instead of waiting her turn."*

Altgeld Hall Ladies' Room, 1900

Jacob Haish Library, 1899

Haish Library Reference and Periodical Section, 1900

Because he had contributed the funds for Northern's first library, the trustees named the library for Jacob Haish; the bust over the fireplace mantel (right center of picture) is that of Haish. This remained Northern's library for over a half-century until the completion of the Swen Parson Library in 1951. The Haish Library consisted of two large rooms on the main floor of the building, one for the reading and reference room and one for the stack or book room. Six windows and a stained-glass skylight lighted the library by day, and electric lights brought light to the night. By the time the library opened to students on January 2, 1900, it boasted a collection of over 5,000 volumes. And, noted the student paper, "through the generosity of Jacob Haish . . . no expense has been spared in the furnishings and fittings." It is interesting to note that DeKalb's current public library is also named for Jacob Haish in honor of his substantial contributions to its creation and development. All this from a man who had very little formal education but greatly appreciated the value of books and reading.

Altgeld Hall Auditorium, 1899

Terraced gardens, the lagoon, the Plant House, and the zoo complemented the Castle's exterior; Altgeld's interior also provided many places for students to explore. In addition to a science laboratory, recitation rooms, and offices, the building offered a state-of-the-art auditorium, a gymnasium, a library, and, within a few years, a lending museum. The auditorium, exquisitely crafted and lit by the still new phenomenon of electric lights, was usually the first port of call for all students and staff each day for general exercises. It was in "gen ex" that the president gave his daily homily, the staff made the announcements for the day, and students madly worked as best they could to complete assignments due in class a few hours later.

"One day I managed to get lost in the northern confines of the Normal building, and I thought surely I had wandered into the engine room of some well-ordered factory, so bewildered was I by all the machinery," one student wrote. "A nice looking man came in and remarked, 'Lost, Freshman?' I don't see why they call us fresh men, neither word is appropriate," she continued. Then the engineer took her on a complete tour, explaining how the dynamo supplied electricity for the five hundred lights in the auditorium and the three hundred other sixteen-candlepower lights scattered throughout the building. He also showed her the air system complete with fans that were operated by electric motors and supplied fresh air to all of the rooms. The unscheduled tour ended with Chief Engineer George Shoop proudly showing her the state-of-the-art boiler system for delivering hot water and heat throughout the large building regulated by thermostatic valves.

The people who make any college or university go are the secretaries, custodians, engineers, mechanics, groundskeepers, and cooks, who feed the students, cut the grass, supply the heat, clean the public rooms, and keep the records. Northern had only one building at the beginning, and the small staff, pictured here, had to do everything, including keeping the boilers and dynamos running so there would be heat and electricity. George Shoop led this group from 1899 until his death in 1915. Shortly after the school opened its doors, the student newspaper ran a brief piece recounting Shoop's attempt to repair a boiler line up near the ceiling: "The fire alarm raised last week caused a little excitement. The cause of it was that Mr. Shoop, in reaching to the stepladder after climbing through a hole in the ceiling, kicked it out from under him. Consequently, as he was hanging by his hands ten feet from the floor, he called for help. This breaking of the customary silence was interpreted to mean that the building was on fire and was by some acted on accordingly. Dr. Cook says, 'The building cannot catch fire; but, if it should, come and report to the office.'"

The Boiler Room, 1900

LYMAN POWELL
Engineer

GEORGE SHOOP
Head Janitor

JAMES MC CANN
Assistant Janitor

FRED REED
Assistant Janitor

ROY CAMP
Night Engineer

JOHN SWAIN
Fireman

All students had to make that end-of-the-day walk back down the hill into town to the rooming houses in which they lived. Wood planks served to keep their feet out of the mud—and to reduce the burden of cleaning the halls of the Castle. Without the modern fibers and garments to protect them from the cold DeKalb winters, students dressed in layers of wool and cotton from head to foot. In this photo, smoke from the wire mills east of downtown hangs over the trees on the horizon.

castle on a hill

O beautiful Kishwaukee, placid stream,
With the wildly rushing waters seen in dream!
On thy early shores the red men came and went,
By the alder trees and birches pitching tent;
Earnest of the might future yet unseen
By the fairy, purple flowers leaved in green.

When the winter snowpack melted, the Kishwaukee River swelled
nearly to the bridge level. Student Minnie Hausen was the first of
many to write a poetic tribute to the Kishwaukee, and she published
it in the student newspaper in 1900.

chapter two

STUDENT LIFE

From the beginning, Northern students organized many extracurricular groups, societies, and clubs. The entire student population divided in two by last name, alphabetically, and joined either the Ellwood or the Glidden Society. These two groups competed throughout the year and put on programs that included oratory, music, theater, and debates on current events. With the faculty as judges, the groups competed for the Perseus Trophy (shown on next page) awarded at the end of the spring term. Eighty percent of the students were female, so it is not surprising that issues important to women often came up in debate. In the first Literary Contest, Minnie M. Bush presented her essay, "The Obligation of Educated Women to the Social Settlement," and Blanch Munson Capron read her paper, "The Growth and Influence of Women's Clubs in America." The programs sometimes featured world events. In the first Ellwood-Glidden contest of the spring of 1900, the debate was titled "Resolved, that the United States Should Not Permanently Retain and Govern the Philippine Islands."

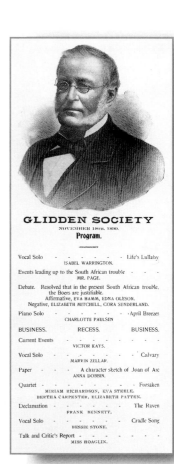

The Perseus Trophy went to the society that had earned the most victories in head-to-head competition during the year.

The Ellwood and Glidden Societies provided cultural and social outlets for the students, including debates, guest lectures, music recitals, and group activities to promote an esprit de corps. The two groups also worked to improve the campus, and the photo at right shows members of the Ellwood Society planting a tree east of Altgeld Hall. The students did much of their practice teaching in the DeKalb Public Schools, and they frequently invited their pupils to campus to participate in extracurricular activities. One favorite each year was the May Day Celebration complete with the Maypole seen in the photo at the top of the next page.

May Fete, the annual festival celebrating the arrival of spring, began in 1900 as the May Day Dance, and it is the oldest annual student activity. From its modest beginnings with a Maypole for area children, it grew quickly into a major undertaking and by the 1920s, enjoyed a queen and her court, theater on the lawn, picnic lunches, athletic games, literary contests, and a formal dance. Pictured above is May Fete Queen and Court, 1922.

The scene of jousting knights in this photo from the 1922 celebration contained a little of everything for the audience.

castle on a hill

Service fraternity Alpha Phi Omega introduced the first tug-of-war to May Fete, as it was then known, in 1951. Most of the activities associated with May Fete took place in the lagoon area, and the tugs traditionally stretched across the water from the island to the shore. Greek fraternities dominated the tugs over the years, but in the mid-1960s, the Flunkies Independent Organization won the event by beating the champions of the three previous years, Alpha Phi Omega. The crowds grew each year, nearing 10,000 by the end of the 1960s. The tugs moved to the stadium in 1968. That year was also the first year for fireworks at May Fete.

By the 1970s, May Fete had transformed into Springfest. Women's tugs became an official event in May of 1971. Today, the tugs go on but have moved out of Springfest and away from the lagoon to Greek Row north of campus. The picture at bottom of previous page is from the 1955 May Fete tugs. In the top picture, taken in 1966, Greek organizations had added chariot races to the activities.

Northern Illinois State Normal
School Band, 1900

Northern Illinois
Orchestra, 1903

Although Northern did not have a formal music department in 1899, mathematics professor Swen Parson soon organized several instrumental and choral groups through which students could express their talents. Parson also regularly performed with his own Swen Parson Trio. Students training to become teachers appreciated the opportunity to gain musical experience that they could take into the classroom later.

The Huskie Marching Band has traveled across America to perform on stages, in parades, and at football games. At bottom, the drum major is leading the band in concert at the California Bowl in December of 1983. The band shed its traditional uniforms in 1975 (see photo above) and became the Huskie Show Band. The Show Band, under the leadership of Michael T. Embrey, changed not only its uniforms but also its style toward jazz and pop music with choreography and color guards to match the new image. In the nineties, the old became new again as the band switched back into the more traditional marching band uniforms they wear in public performance today. The band provides opportunities for music and nonmusic majors alike to continue their music education and to perform in public. No basketball or football game would have the same level of energy without the pep band spirit.

Northern students have always enthusiastically participated in the performing arts. Music, theater, and dance groups attracted students who would practice, give public performances and recitals, and also participate in larger annual events such as Homecoming, May Fete, and commencement. Performing arts often spilled outside the grandeur of the Altgeld Hall Auditorium. The photo at the top depicts a choral ensemble on stilts photographed just outside Altgeld in 1909. A close inspection of the photograph suggests this was a mixed group of male and female students. In the fall and spring, groups often took advantage of the well-manicured lawn and terraces to the south of Altgeld Hall for outdoor performances.

Goldilocks and the Bears, 1927

Above is a photograph of one of the Shakespearean plays performed on the terraced lawns to the immediate south of the building in 1915. In her review of the play, Charlotte Sheehan said, "Four centuries had been taken from time. Spectators beheld beauty and mirthful revelers. Modern styles were forgotten to give way to kingly robes and plumes. Gorgeous costumes and rare laces and satins graced the womanly figures. The gayety of the past was a thing of the present, and in the old, old take that is ever new, the senior class made 'Much Ado About Nothing.'" [Note the character lurking in the bushes.]

For over one hundred years, students have kept theater alive and well on the campus and annually provide audiences comedies, musicals, mysteries, and drama in plays old and new. At left is a scene from Picket Fences, a recent, award-winning play about race relations in America during World War II. This NIU performance took place in 1996.

Orchesis Dance Troop, 1934

Orchesis, an organization formed for the purpose of stimulating interest in dance as an art form, became a favorite activity at Northern in the 1930s. Nine women interested in physical training and dance founded the group in 1929, and it remained an important part of cultural and social life on campus for the next forty years. By the 1970s, dance had become an integral part of the physical education curriculum. But in the 1930s, Orchesis was a social group in which "individuality and cooperation meet on a common ground; for each girl is allowed to work out her own ideas, while all help in the expression of those ideas through the dance." Sixty years later, Orchesis had become part of Northern's history and the Department of Theater and Dance offered more than a dozen different dance classes per semester. Pictured at left is an Orchesis dancer in a 1997 performance. Mirroring the arrival of high technology at the end of the twentieth century are the Cyborg Dancers below.

Dance as physical training and art has a long history at Northern, but dance as social activity goes back to the very beginnings. Annual activities such as the celebration of Christmas, Winter Fest, Sadie Hawkins Day, and May Fete usually had a formal dance as one of the centerpiece activities. In an era when few students commuted, there was no television, and life was slower, these annual activities were the core of a student's social life at Northern. One of the annual favorites in the 1920s was the dance held on Washington's Birthday in February. In December of 1920, two weeks before the end of the fall term, student leaders proposed a so-called single tax for the support of student activities. President Brown called for a vote. The students voted unanimously to pay a self-imposed fee of one dollar per term to support social activities. Thus was born the mandatory student fee. The photograph at left shows the Washington Birthday Dance from 1922 held in the Altgeld Hall gymnasium.

The second oldest tradition at Northern is the annual Homecoming celebration in October. In Northern's earliest years, the centerpiece was simply the gathering of alumni at a social event to renew acquaintance and catch up on what had happened to friends after graduation. Soon enough, however, the football game between alums and the current team found a place on the weekend agenda, then a dance in addition to the dinner, and finally a parade on Saturday to complement the afternoon's football game. In the 1920s, the parade tradition of winding through downtown DeKalb to the campus began. The Northern Illinois Fine Arts Club entered this rather elaborately decorated horse and wagon (left) in the 1929 parade and won first prize for best entry by a group.

Antiquity themes seemed to be very popular over the years, and the float at the right, titled "It's Greek to Me," won best entry in the 1955 Homecoming Parade. According to the Norther, "the judges had a difficult decision to make and then came the results. After shouts of congratulation and excited laughter subsided, everyone heard the news. Pi Kappa Sigma and Theta Kappa Phi took top honors." The rise of the Greek system on campus in the 1950s strengthened all aspects of the Homecoming weekend, especially the parade and the parties after the big game.

In 1949, Northern was in the midst of celebrating its fiftieth, golden, anniversary. The theme for Homecoming that year was "Forward Look," and students elected Florence Allison Homecoming Queen. While most of the floats followed the theme of looking forward, the float at the right won the greatest applause on the parade route. A Waterman veteran created this replica of the battleship Illinois to honor all those who had fought in World War II, especially Navy veterans. He entered the float in many local parades over several years. The large influx of men returning from military service swelled enrollment by 400 percent at Northern between 1944 and 1949. Northern's "Huskies snarled their way to victory over the fighting Hurons of Michigan Normal, 39–14" that year. Alpha Sigma Alpha's "Dream Pipe" float won best entry in the 1949 parade.

Off-campus groups, too, created parade entries. In the case in the bottom photo, the driver apparently forgot to check the gas tank before starting off on the 1957 Homecoming Parade route.

Student life featured other annual events beyond Homecoming and May Fete. Stunt Night, Winter Carnival, Christmas Formal Dance, Alpha Phi Omega's Ugliest Man on Campus Contest, the Valentine's Day Dance, and an annual Sadie Hawkins Day Dance were extremely popular in the 1950s.

Sadie Hawkins Day was one of the most popular of these annual events and gave women a chance to take the lead and ask a guy during a time when such behavior would normally have been frowned upon. Sadie Hawkins Day came out of the "Li'l Abner" comic strip created by Al Capp in 1934. In the fictional town of Dogpatch, the mayor, Hekzebiah Hawkins, had a daughter so ugly she could not attract a mate. So the mayor formally declared a day when the females could chase the males and any male caught would have to marry the female catching him. Capp had no idea this would catch on when the first official Sadie Hawkins Day was celebrated on November 9, 1938. Within two years, colleges across the country had appropriated the idea to give the women a chance to take the initiative. Northern held its first Sadie Hawkins Day March 9, 1940, but for most of the next twenty years, the event was held in October or November. By the early sixties, it had run its course and died a natural death. In the photo at left, you can see that participants dressed to the rural Appalachian Dogpatch–style.

The third major dance of the fall term in the 1950s was the annual Christmas Formal. The big band era had energized formal dances held in the main women's dormitory at Northern, Williston Hall. The swing bands that carried over into the fifties from the forties were about to give way to the new bebop and hop bands of the mid-fifties, the predecessors to the rock-and-roll of the sixties. Bands like Bill Haley and the Comets and The Champs and a hot new crooner named Elvis Presley rapidly changed the pop music scene. Still, in a survey of college students taken in the fall of 1956, less than 40 percent said yes when asked: "Do you enjoy listening to Elvis Presley?" The Northern Star ran an article titled "Collegiate Critics Still Undecided About Elvis" that same year, but the foundation for the rock revolution had already been laid.

When the annual Christmas Formal dances died, the medieval madrigal dinners rose to take their place in the pantheon of favorite Northern annual events. In the photo above, trumpeters Rick Radek, Bill Schlacko, and Vic Donnell serenade the diners in the big ballroom of the Holmes Student Center. The first Madrigal Dinner was held in the ballroom of the Holmes Student Center on December 15, 1964, and 500 attended. Fourteen student singers introduced each course with a song related to the food being served, and a trumpet fanfare introduced the singers. The courses were standard "Old English viands" of roast beef, complete with a wassail bowl, boar's head, and flaming pudding. The singers wore costumes authentic to the Elizabethan period that were replicated from museum examples and created by other students in the NIU Home Economics Club. More than 250 yards of satin and velvet fabric went into the costumes. Interest grew so quickly that by 1969 the dinner had expanded to six nights with 400 guests per night with the first evening being a formal wear event. After a twenty-five-year run, interest in the dinners began to diminish, but they will always have a place as part of Northern's history.

First established in 1945 at the suggestion of retired math professor Swen Parson, Winter Carnival soon became an established annual event. The biggest problem over the years was the lack of cooperation by the weather: too much mud and too little ice and snow. Winter Carnival took place after the semester break sometime in January or February, and a week of activities included a snow sculpture contest, ice skating competition, snowshoe races, a concert, a faculty show, and a midway of booths. Until 1968, students elected the Snow Queen by popular vote. Then, judges selected the queen in a pageant modeled on the Miss America Pageant. By 1969, men, too, competed in pageant-like events to become the Snow King. Some campus organizations used Winter Carnival as a fundraiser, and generally tickets sold for a dime. The 1968 Winter Carnival sold 37,000 tickets, by far the largest number ever. By the 1970s, interest died, and the last-recorded NIU Winter Carnival took place in 1972.

Crowning the Winter Carnival Queen, Kay Piazza, 1959

castle on a hill

Williston Hall, Northern's first dormitory, opened to women residents in 1915 and remained the only dormitory on campus for over thirty years. With the rapid expansion of enrollment after World War II, a second dorm for women, Adams Hall, opened in 1949. The men continued to find space in DeKalb homes and in Vetville, and a few DeKalb residents converted their garages to short-term shelter for the returning heroes of World War II. Not until 1951 would the first residence hall for men open on campus, Gilbert Hall. Throughout much of Northern's history, most of the student's social life was tied to residence hall living. The late-night card parties, weekend mixers, outdoor picnics, and small parties in the recreation rooms complemented the big annual social events such as Homecoming, Sadie Hawkins Day, and the Christmas Formal. Under the scrutiny of residence hall personnel, the women socialized with men in the large first-floor lounge of Williston Hall seen in this 1917 photo above.

The basement recreation room substituted for the family living room, and in the photo at left, four Adams Hall residents gathered round the piano to sing a few songs and enjoy a Coca-Cola.

It is the important little details of life in the dorm that often seem to stick most in the memories of alumni. Many students have not lived away from home before, and life's little essentials like doing the laundry and checking the mail each day become important. These three photos date from 1979. One major change students seem to have difficulty adjusting to in residence hall life is the communal bathroom.

Dorm living requires most students to adjust to much smaller living space than they had at home. This was especially true in the years right after the end of World War II. Enrollment grew so fast in the late 1940s that Williston Hall put beds into the attic to accommodate the new arrivals. Even if it was only a bed, each student tried to make it home with the personalized bulletin board hung above the headboard. The opening of Adams Hall in 1949 took the pressure off for the women, at least.

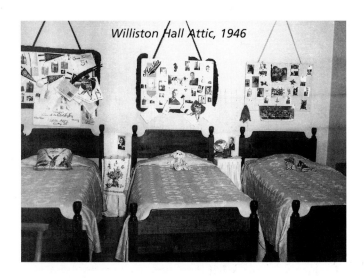

Williston Hall Attic, 1946

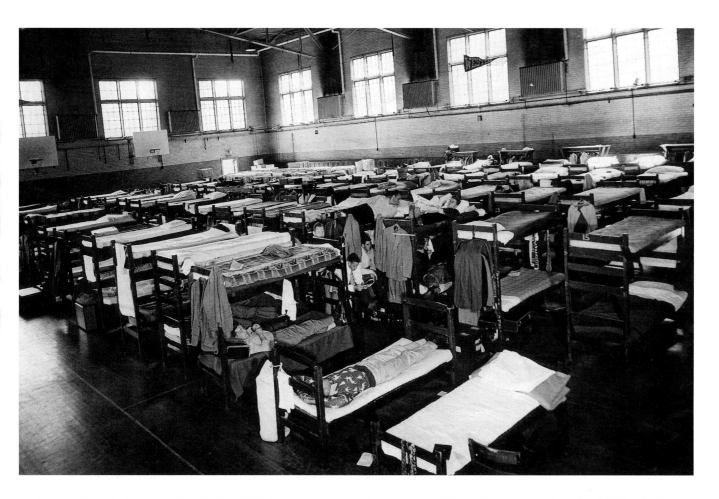

As fast as enrollment had plummeted from 1941 to 1943, it rose even faster once the war was over. Of the 445 on campus in the spring of 1945, only 48 were men; just one year later, total enrollment had climbed to 750 with 308 men. And 255 of the 308 men were veterans. In the fall of 1947, enrollment hit a record 1,700, almost a 400 percent increase in just two years. One of the first problems to solve in this explosion was to find housing. Federal statutes guaranteeing educational benefits and housing support underwrote a tidal wave of returning G.I.'s to the nation's campuses. In many cases, these returning vets differed from the Normal student of just a few years earlier. Many were in their twenties, some were married, some had children in tow. Temporary barracks from Camp McCoy in Wisconsin found their way to DeKalb and became known as Vetville, a large complex just north of Lucinda Avenue and the main campus buildings. These temporary buildings lasted nearly forty years until the last was torn down in the 1980s. Single men found themselves crammed into Still Gym and virtually any other place where bunks could be erected. Somewhat used to the crowding on ships, in tents, and at military facilities, the tight conditions did not deter these men from coming back to school.

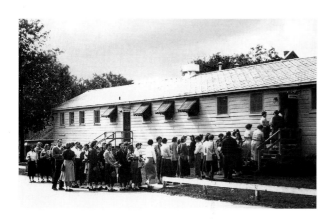

Preparing the thousands of meals each day for those living in the barracks also posed a challenge. Navy veteran Bumpy Smith remembered that there were temporary quarters for "married couples, too." And not all vets took their meals in the cafeteria pictured in the left photo, situated north of Altgeld Hall. Smith remembered moving into a temporary apartment created within a barracks where "there were two rooms, and then a middle bathroom and two more rooms, and two guys in each room, so there were four guys in each unit. . . . We started to share cooking, and we had hot-plates, and each guy had one day to cook a meal."

✠ Proudly We Hail ✠

Lt. Stanton W. Johnston
U. S. Army Air Force
Killed on Duty April 4, 1943

Capt. Merle C. Eby
U. S. Army Air Force
Missing in Action June 26, 1943

Lt. Rayfield E. Edwards
U. S. Army Air Force
Killed on Duty March 27, 1943

Lt. Harold C. Cook
U. S. Army Air Force
Missing in Action February 16, 1943

Lt. Gideon Warne
U. S. Army Air Force
Missing in Action March 22, 1943

John Borner
U. S. Army
Killed in Action July 27, 1943

By the time Victory in Europe Day came on May 8, 1945, twenty-five former Northern students had died and another fifteen were listed as missing in action or prisoners of war. Many of the survivors had been wounded. Le Roy Davison, a boxer and member of the 1940 U.S. Olympic team, traded his hero's gold for a hero's purple heart. Davison first flew sorties over Germany from bases in England before shipping out for the South Pacific. Shot down over a remote island, Davison hid in the jungle for almost a month. He didn't have much food, and he couldn't move because he had been shot in the leg, according to the Northern Illinois. He doctored himself and stayed alive until friendly troops evacuated him to safety. Those who survived returned home to crowded college campuses seeking to build the foundation for a better life in the future. The pictures at the left appeared in the October 1, 1943, edition of the student newspaper in tribute to the fallen heroes.

Williston Weekend Travelers, 1936

Although no student owned a car when Northern first opened in 1899, thirty years later, the first student-driven vehicles began to appear on the campus. With the advent of cheaper, more accessible mass transit and the growth of the automobile in American society, the Northern "tradition" of commuting home for the weekend established itself in the 1930s. Ever since, there has always been a Friday night exodus from DeKalb as students sought home-cooked food, clean laundry, and time with family and friends. Cars, interurban trolleys, trains, and buses transported those who thought weekend life in DeKalb too dull. And, predictably, once students began to leave on the weekends, those remaining complained there was no one left with whom to party. Train service did come out to DeKalb from Chicago until it ceased in the 1970s.

Not everyone, however, found DeKalb boring or lacking in parties. This student at right, pictured in the 1937 Norther, seemed to have found himself a good time though he did manage to keep his garters up.

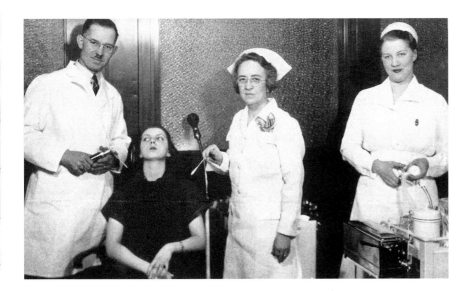

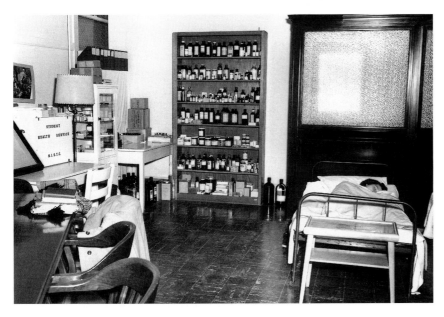

Martha Newcomb, 1916

With the opening of Williston Hall as the first campus dormitory, Northern hired its first health professional to provide care for the students. Martha Newcomb, trained at Baptist Hospital in Chicago, came to Northern from Earlham College in Indiana. Over the years, the student demand for health services escalated, and a separate fee per credit hour underwrote the expansion to fill the needs. Today, there are over seventy full-time people who work in University Health Services.

The growth in enrollment during the Great Depression brought the establishment of a Health Service in the fall of 1935. President Adams hired Dr. L. V. Burkett to head the new Department of Student Health. Burkett had been head of health services for the Akron, Ohio, public school district. Remodeling of several rooms on the second floor of the Administration Building created a reception room, a doctor's office, an examination room, and two treatment rooms. When Dr. Burkett left after his first year, Adams hired Dr. Lewis Benash to replace him in the fall of 1936. Dr. Benash is shown in photo at top with a very apprehensive student and nurses Donalda Morrison and Miriam Pope.

For those students who were left feeling a bit under the weather, there was always the Health Services. Each day, students came through the doors with an amazing variety of flus, colds, sprains, fractures, abrasions, cuts, and a few ailments and injuries rarely seen. Until the 1960s, facilities were rather limited and sparse as can be seen in this 1954 photograph (bottom left). With not so much as a locker in which to put her coat, the student simply tossed her books on the table, hung her coat on the chair, and climbed into bed to sleep it off. In a scene that would cause health practitioners today to faint, the entire supply of drugs, astringents, and assorted dressings is available should the student need something to help her through whatever ailed her.

THE TOWERS

1939

Towers *First Edition, 1939*

As the Great Depression moved toward an end and the clouds of war rose over Europe, Northern students established a literary publication. The Towers would become the benchmark for quality for all student publications. Although World War II interrupted annual publication from 1941 to 1946, Towers returned after the war and today is still the best literary production on campus each year. Over the past sixty years, the publication has won numerous national awards for student literary journals, and many of its contributors have gone on to careers in writing and teaching English and American literature. This literary magazine became one of the three campus publications that would stand the test of time. The others were the annual yearbook, the Norther, and, of course, the student newspaper now known as the Northern Star.

From that very first semester, the student newspaper has been an important part of student life on the campus. Even before the opening of classes in 1899, students began to organize a newspaper. They produced a commemorative newspaper for the opening of the school in September 1899 and ran 1,500 copies to be given out as souvenirs. The first regular newspaper, called the Northern Illinois, came out of General Exercises on October 20, 1899, where it was christened by Dr. Cook and nursed by Alice Crosby and W. R. Lloyd, editor and assistant editor, under the counsel of Fred L. Charles. The paper included a social events column, a humor page, photographs, and literary pieces, as well as campus and town news. Single copies sold for ten cents and a yearly subscription for fifty cents. Students also produced an excellent yearbook annually, the Norther, beginning in 1900. Taken together, the two student publications are now the best source of information on the first half-century of Northern's history since no official archives existed until 1964. The yearbook provided many of the photographs found in the pages at hand. Pictured in the photo below is the Northern Illinois staff from 1900.

"The Board of Managers has not neglected the duty of providing a home for the Northern Illinois. It is [in] a pleasant south room in the Normal building [now Altgeld Hall]. The walls are tinted two shades of delicate green." The staff also solicited input from students noting, "a news box for voluntary contributions may be found on the table. All are invited to make use of it as a receptacle for literary output, local events, entertaining verse, side-splitting barbs, and so forth." In the early years, the newspaper published student fiction, poetry, and jokes, as well as gossipy news notes about faculty. The paper published only monthly at first. Professor Fred L. Charles agreed to be the first faculty adviser and student Alice Crosby, the first editor. The first printed photograph in the paper did not appear until March 19, 1931, and the first summer editions in 1937.

Northern Illinois *Press Room, 1911*

For the first few decades, students printed the paper on the campus in a room not far from the paper's offices. Today, the printing is contracted out off campus.

Through the years, the newspaper has had its share of conflicts with university administrators, and it has built an enviable alumni network that can be brought to its defense when necessary. Among the many memorable front pages is this one at far left announcing the end of Richard Nelson's tenure as president of Northern. The newspaper itself was at the center of the storm that brought an end to Clyde Wingfield's presidency in the spring of 1986.

National and international events came to the campus on the front page of the morning paper, too, as seen in this memorable cover at left from January 17, 1991.

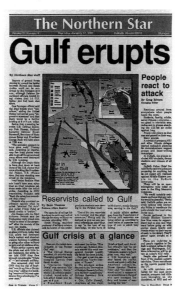

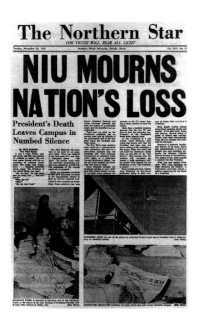

What December 7 was for the World War II Generation and September 11 for Generation X, November 22 was for the Baby Boom Generation. Every person who was on the Northern campus that day in 1963 can tell you where she was and what she was doing when she heard the news: "The president is dead." The magnitude of the assassination seemed to suspend time, and history changed in some way that day for each person in America. For a shocked nation and world it seemed as if Camelot itself had died. The killing marked another end of innocence in a decade that would see many more violent events.

The bright promise of Kennedy's election in 1960 began the decade, and the violent protests that swept Northern's campus in the spring of 1970 ended it. These ten years would be known by future generations simply as "The Sixties." It was equal to the twenties as a decade that brought significant and permanent changes in the American social milieu. In a very tangible sense, the echoes of what started in the sixties can be seen on the periphery of the Northern campus today in the Women's Studies Center and the Center for Black Studies on the south, the Latino Studies Center on the north, the Social Sciences Research Center on the east, and the huge, sprawling recreation complex on the west. All find their roots in "The Sixties."

Until 1968, Northern, like most colleges and universities, had gender-segregated dormitories and rules for social behavior that mirrored those found in many middle-class homes of the time. These included a curfew of 10:00 p.m. on weekday nights for women to be in the dorm before housemothers locked the doors for the evening. Thus was born the nightly ritual of couples congregating around the entrances of women's dorms saying their fond farewells. Sorority and town rooming houses enforced the same rules, and a dean of men and dean of women watched over the welfare of students. The policy of in loco parentis fell at college after college in the mid-sixties, and, finally, in June of 1968, Northern abandoned all curfews for women. Curfew had always been a double standard with men's hours not circumscribed as were those of women. Northern's administrators eliminated curfew hours for women April 18, 1968, and abolished the dean positions in 1972. One of the most frequent arguments heard by students' rights advocates was that if, at age eighteen, one was old enough to vote, to be drafted, and to die for one's country, surely eighteen-year-olds could manage their own private lives. As the decade wore on and the draft began to heat up for the war in Vietnam that argument took on more meaning.

Last Kiss, Neptune Hall, 1962

Hair, especially long hair, was one of the bellwether issues of the sixties. In the fifties, the effects of World War II were still seen in both men and women whose hair was short and well groomed. The flattop or buzz cut had come to prominence during the war to reduce scalp disease and allow easy (or no) care. Here, a student visits one of DeKalb's longtime businesses, the Sanitary Barber Shop, on East Lincoln Highway for his haircut. All-American Al Eck flashes his big smile under the haircut of choice for the football team, the flattop. Eck earned small college All-American honors.

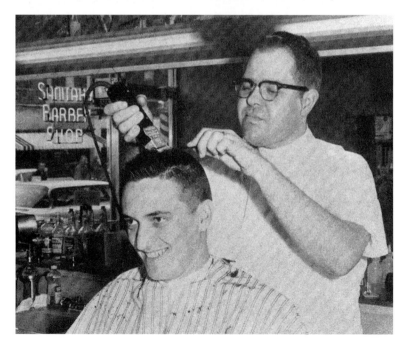

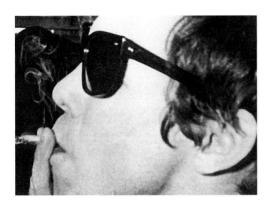

As the 1960s wore on, hairstyles lengthened each year. Pop culture icons, particularly rock musicians, especially influenced male hairstyles. The Beatles introduced the mop top to American teens with their arrival in 1963, and by the end of the decade, many male students had shoulder-length hair while female students had hair well below the shoulder in length. And, as in this photo, marijuana had joined alcohol and tobacco as a drug of choice for many students. The symbolic import of hair length and style was such that the rock opera musical simply titled Hair became a major Broadway hit.

Another rising cultural phenomenon of the 1960s was Chicago publisher Hugh Hefner's Playboy magazine. Once Hefner built his magazine into a pop culture force, he created a string of Playboy Clubs across the country and then laid out what he called the Playboy philosophy in his magazine. Students on many college campuses took him seriously, and in dormitories, cafeterias, student unions, and campus ministries, Northern students discussed the rapidly changing ethics of sexuality and gender in America. While Hefner may not have influenced sexual behavior so much as reflected those changes, his magazine did set the tone for style and clothing fashion on campus in the sixties. Campus ministries met the rise of the Playboy philosophy head on with informal study discussion groups often held in impromptu coffee houses.

There was plenty of fun and fluff in student activities outside the classroom. Where earlier generations had swallowed goldfish and danced without cease for days, this generation opted for seeing how many students could be stuffed into telephone booths and automobiles. The Volkswagen Beetle was a favorite for stuffing on many campuses, but at Northern, the group below decided to try an International Harvester Scout.

Greek Row Chariot Races, 1960

While some sororities stuffed Scouts, others participated in Greek and Roman games. Sorority chariot races not only won laureates for the winners, they often also raised money for charities. One of the favorite activities of the decade was the Roman toga party later made famous in the movie Animal House. The hedonism of the Playboy philosophy melded well with the Roman-themed parties. Active chapters of several national sororities and fraternities were on the campus in the 1950s, but it was in the sixties that the growth took place to the north of the campus that became known as Greek Row.

Thirty years later, the annual Greek Physique contest had come to be one of the favored annual activities harking back to the Greek ideal of a well-educated mind in the perfectly developed body. Here, Northern Star photographer Sam Summers captured one of the winning poses by Chris Pope who represented Delta Upsilon in the 1998 contest. Both men and women participated in the annual body builders pageant held in the Holmes Student Center.

Beginning in the mid-fifties, Northern experienced another ten-year period of explosive enrollment growth as it had right after World War II. And once again the complexion of the campus changed significantly. The general prosperity of America in the sixties combined with a new national agenda of positive social change to bring record numbers of Hispanic, Asian, and African American students to the campus. With their arrival, they brought new organizations, including the first active local chapters of historically black fraternities and sororities. In the above photo, the men of Alpha Kappa Psi that joined the NIU campus April 28, 1968, posed in the Huskie's Den of the then new Holmes Student Center. They, too, sported the longer Afro hairstyle popular in the sixties.

The first Black sorority on campus was the Delta Omicron Chapter of Alpha Kappa Alpha that received its charter May 22, 1960. This group had existed as a local sorority, Tau Delta Sigma, since January 12, 1959. The above picture was taken in 1970.

Black Choir, 1969

With the increase in the number of African American students came the opportunity to expand the musical horizons at Northern. In 1969, the new Black Choir raised every voice in song and brought audiences out of their seats with the up-tempo gospel sound that would become its trademark in the coming decades.

Fanny Ruth Patterson from Hinckley, Illinois, was the first African American to graduate from Northern back in 1915. Fanny had completed high school, worked for a few years, then, at the age of twenty-one, came to complete the two-year college program. When she completed her degree at Northern, President John Cook wrote a letter of recommendation for her to the head of personnel for the St. Louis schools, Ben Blewett. Fanny, Cook wrote, "is an excellent girl, having good looks, good taste, extreme modesty of demeanor, and a good mind." He recommended her for a position teaching English and history, concluding his letter by saying, "she is a most excellent and interesting young woman and she has had the entire confidence of everybody with whom she has worked." Sadly, Fanny died of pulmonary tuberculosis February 17, 1920, at the young age of twenty-seven years, six months, three days. Her life, though short, remains an important part of NIU history.

When the Kennedy administration targeted racially segregated public southern universities, students across America debated the issues and, in many cases, held rallies to support Kennedy's initiative. The rally pictured here from 1962 was the first of many large, outdoor rallies on the NIU campus in favor of civil rights. When the civil rights legislation of the Johnson administration came into force, the movement gained steam, and there were some freedom riders from Northern who went into the South to help to educate and register black voters. The newly arrived pastors of the Baptist Campus Ministry, John and Ruth Peterson, were among them. It was that ministry that would become the first black Christian community in DeKalb. The Petersons' foundation eventually became the New Hope Baptist Church of DeKalb in the 1990s.

At a time of heightened race consciousness, many NIU black students had begun to sit together at athletic events, and some refused to stand for the national anthem, choosing instead to express their protest with a raised, clenched fist. President Richard Nelson, just five months in office, decided to defuse the tension at basketball games by not playing the national anthem. His attempt to bring peace only brought more antagonism from outside the university, and soon the letters and telegrams poured into the president's office. A telegram from Georgia Lieutenant Governor Lester Maddox was typical: "[Y]ou have helped to bring America to one of the darkest hours in all her glorious history. No patriotic and freedom loving American would dare suggest that the Star Spangled Banner be outlawed at any time or place upon the soul of this great nation. . . . Your position is deplorable, intolerable, and Un-American." Note the one who marched to a different drummer in the top left of this photograph. Freedom of speech prevailed.

Political protest at Northern had not been common during the first sixty years, but there were roots to what would become the student activism of the 1960s. Already in the post–World War II years, students successfully led a boycott of downtown DeKalb restaurants that refused to serve African American patrons. And thirty years before that, women students on the campus joined in the national crusade for suffrage as seen in the photo at right shot outside Williston Hall in 1917.

Suffragettes at Northern, 1917

Vietnam War Protestor, 1967

As the civil rights protests on campus gained steam through the sixties, the antiwar movement also called students from their classrooms and dormitories out to march, sing, and take a stand. Soon enough, the flyers would be posted, the speakers would take the bullhorn, and the rally would begin. And many times, the protests were aimed as much against the corporations profiting from the Vietnam War as the military, the draft, or the administration prosecuting the war.

The student rights and free speech movements swept across American campuses in the 1960s, and several rather loosely organized groups seemed always to be in the center of protests and marches. The Students for a Democratic Society (SDS) drew more than a little resistance from those who saw it as the agent of the new left favoring changes that would undermine traditional society. When Dow Chemical's recruiters came to the NIU Placement Office in Lowden Hall in February of 1967, protesters with picket signs (left) met them. Dow, manufacturer of the napalm used to incinerate villages and people in Vietnam, found pickets in its path on most of the campuses it visited.

On Northern's campus, students regularly gathered to march in Chicago as well as in DeKalb, and by 1970, the protestors' message was one and it was clear: end the war. Ohio National Guardsmen shot and killed students on the Kent State campus May 4. On May 5, protesting NIU students found themselves with a curfew after they smashed a number of downtown windows. Police arrested thirty-seven. The next day, President Smith canceled classes for May 7 and 8, and the Illinois National Guard was put on alert for possible deployment to DeKalb. A week later, on May 11, Augusta, Georgia, police shot and killed six black protestors, and two black students at Jackson State died when fired upon. Once again, the civil rights and antiwar movements had intersected, and the deaths precipitated violence on the NIU campus. Although there were no serious personal injuries with the student demonstrations of May 1970, property damage mounted, and the potential for a disaster was near at hand. Protest fever peaked the night of May 18. Milwaukee activist Father James Groppi ignited the flame with a rousing speech condemning the slaughter of the black protesters in Georgia: all had been shot in the back. After a protest march across the campus following Groppi, most students dispersed, but several hundred continued to hold forth in the free speech area outside Watson East. Around midnight, they headed across campus for downtown where police were waiting in force. President Rhoten Smith put himself between the protesters and the police and townspeople on the east side of the Lincoln Highway Bridge to prevent violence. Police finally waded into the group at 3:00 a.m. and arrested thirty people. But the guns remained unfired, and Smith had averted a Kent State or Jackson State disaster. Smith declared another two-day moratorium on classes, and the protestors' ardor finally began to cool. The crisis had passed.

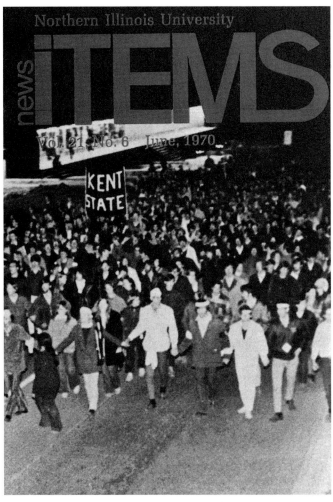

At many large universities, underground student newspapers came to be part of the scene, and NIU was no exception. The most important and longest-lived was News From Nowhere; the cover of the first edition is seen here.

Montgomery
Arboretum
Protest, 1971

As student activism reached its zenith in the early 1970s, a new course was added to the civil rights and antiwar menu, the despoiling of the ecology. Students often targeted major American corporations and public institutions, especially universities. The protesters wanted some assurance the world they would inherit as older adults would be fit to live in. The NIU administration suggested that the little arboretum just west of the lagoon be removed for parking lot expansion. Student protestors began what would be a successful effort to at least curtail the damage to the green space. In the photo here, a student has chained himself to a tree and two University Police standing in the bucket of a front-end loader are attempting to remove him.

Jesse Jackson at NIU, 1971

Many student protests sought to enlist celebrities to advance the cause, and there were some high-profile activists who established national speaking tours of college campuses. Above, a young Chicago-area preacher, Jesse Jackson, sat waiting his turn to address Northern students in 1971. The NIU International Club and the Wesley Foundation sponsored Jackson's visit. Referring to the politics of the time, Jackson told students: "We are all trapped in the belly of the great white whale, Moby Dick Nixon. Nobody's gonna save us but us." And he preached his own take on race relations: "Both races must learn to live together or perish apart as fools. We started late but the future demands that we arrive on time." To those African American students in the audience, Jackson had a special message: "If black people are going to get well, you must become doctors and heal, you must come home being able to build and construct." Jackson returned for a second visit to NIU February 21, 1987, as a featured speaker for Black History Month.

The parade of area political celebrities that began in the 1970s continued on for the next thirty years as students brought both mainstream and fringe, conservative and radical political voices to the Northern podium. Chicago's only African American mayor, Harold Washington (top left), paid a visit in 1984, and Nation of Islam Minister Louis Farrakhan (bottom left) has made several visits to Northern in the past twenty years. "Chicago," Washington told his audience, "is going to come into the twentieth century if I have to hog-tie and drag it." Unfortunately, he did not live long enough to make good on his promise.

Farrakhan's first NIU appearance brought controversy. The Hillel Jewish Student Association protested that $10,000 in Student Association funds should not be used to, in their words, "bring a racist to this campus." Several hundred people did attend an antiracism rally at noon in the Martin Luther King Commons the day of Farrakhan's visit. Tight security met those attending his speech that evening, and his speech included a defense against the charges of anti-Semitism.

Celebrities from other areas of American life, especially sports and entertainment, joined politicos on the NIU stage. Bill Cosby, Alex Haley, Julian Bond, Wynton Marsalis, Spike Lee, Bill Russell, and a host of others followed in the steps of one of the best known of all twentieth-century celebrities, Muhammad Ali. Known as Cassius Clay when he won the Olympic Gold Medal as a heavyweight boxer in Rome in 1960, Clay converted to Islam, changed his name to Muhammad Ali, and then refused induction into the U.S. Army for service during the Vietnam War. For that, he was stripped of his heavyweight boxing title. While he was waiting a court decision on his refusal to serve in the military, he visited Northern November 15, 1967. Long before Minister Farrakhan came to Northern, Ali brought the message of the Nation of Islam to black students. In a meeting sponsored by the NIU Afro-American Cultural Organization that was open only to black students, Ali presented the message of Islam to about two hundred in attendance. After the meeting, Ali said, "I'll never fight again. More important than boxing is cleaning up our own neighborhoods." Later, in an informal street session, Ali signed autographs, rhymed for the crowd, and then disappeared into his gold Cadillac. The photo at right is Ali with Northern Star *sports reporter Gary Stein.*

Many world-class musicians have performed at NIU but none more accomplished than Wynton Marsalis, seen here at NIU in 1996. Al Hirt had been here in the seventies, the Chicago Symphony regularly visited in the seventies, and Duke Ellington's band played its last public performance with the Duke at the baton in the ballroom of the Holmes Student Center. Marsalis, a consummate artist in the worlds of classical, jazz, and pop music came to Northern at the request of music professor Ron Carter. He gave a free lecture and performance in the Evans Field House and offered a master class for advanced trumpet students in the School of Music. When asked by a student for the best advice he had been given, Marsalis replied, "The best advice I had was from my father and that was to take all the gigs. I played at polka parties, bar mitzvahs, and dances. Music comes out of life."

William the Goose in Jail, 1976

William the Goose. Few human-interest stories surpassed that of Northern's most famous unofficial mascot, William the Goose—and his mate, Wilma—in the late 1970s. Long a fixture of the lagoon goose community, William was special and knew it. Clara Sperling, his closest friend, fed and nurtured him and his mate, Wilma, for years. But the NIU grounds crew wanted to move William out for the winter, and suddenly the Associated Press picked up this picture of William in jail, separated from his beloved Wilma. Chicago columnist Mike Royko wrote about him, the AP sent the picture out worldwide, and William was soon a celebrity. The worst, however, was yet to come. On April 12, 1981, a student killed William, strangling him with a shoelace while he (the student) was under the influence of alcohol and drugs. The student claimed he was simply sleeping it off under a bush when William first attacked him, but there were no credible witnesses to substantiate the student's allegation. Again, William made the AP wires from coast to coast, and clippings came in from such outposts as Yakima, Washington, and East Liverpool, Ohio. This was the last chapter in a tragic story: an unidentified wild dog had killed Wilma the previous summer. William's confidant and friend, Clara Sperling, led the campaign to mount a bronze plaque on a large fieldstone near the east lagoon honoring his memory and designating him an honorary student. His legacy is well told in the several hundred pages of clippings and testimonies found in the NIU Archives. NIU photographer Barry Stark took the picture at the left.

1952 Commencement

The end of the long journey of each student's life at Northern is, paradoxically, called the beginning, commencement. Graduation day arrives, faculty members confer the degree, the student says farewell to friends and then moves out into the world of work. Until the 1960s, one of the annual traditions at Northern was spring commencement at the lagoon. The tradition had begun when students convinced President Adams in 1942 that an outdoor ceremony at the lagoon would be a good idea. While the first effort went well, holding the ceremony outside left much to the vagaries of the late spring weather. Several times, a rainstorm interrupted the ceremony, and the faculty and graduates had to sprint up the hill and out of the storm to the backup site in Still Gymnasium. Finally, in 1957, President Holmes wrote to one of the guest speakers that "for the first time we will be able to have seats available for everyone in case of rain because we will have the new physical education building for men" as the backup site. The size of the graduating class had long since passed the capacity of Still Gym and now, with the opening of the new Evans Field House, Northern had a nice place that could accommodate the ever-larger graduating classes. The growth of the fifties brought the end of the pastoral lagoon commencement ceremonies. Commencement ceremonies today take place in the Convocation Center on the far west side of the campus.

May 1978 Graduate

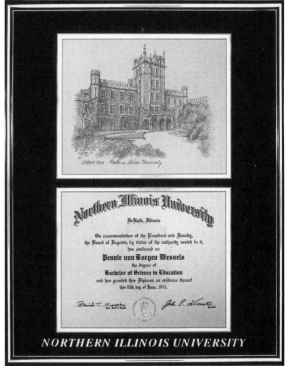

NORTHERN ILLINOIS UNIVERSITY

Adding to the size of commencement was the institution of the graduate programs at Northern in 1951. Dean J. R. Hainds awarded the first Master of Science in Education to Ms. Constance Bax on June 1, 1952, in the lagoon ceremonies. Hainds, Northern's first Director of Graduate Studies, had earned his doctorate at Northwestern and been a member of the English Department faculty since 1940. In 1955, Northern's Board authorized the granting of the Arts Bachelor and Bachelor of Science degrees, marking the first time degrees outside of education could be conferred.

At long last, the moment comes when the officiate calls the graduates to attention and gives the order to move the tassel across the cap signifying they have now completed the degree. All the work, all the expenses, all the late nights, and all the sacrifices now seem worthwhile.

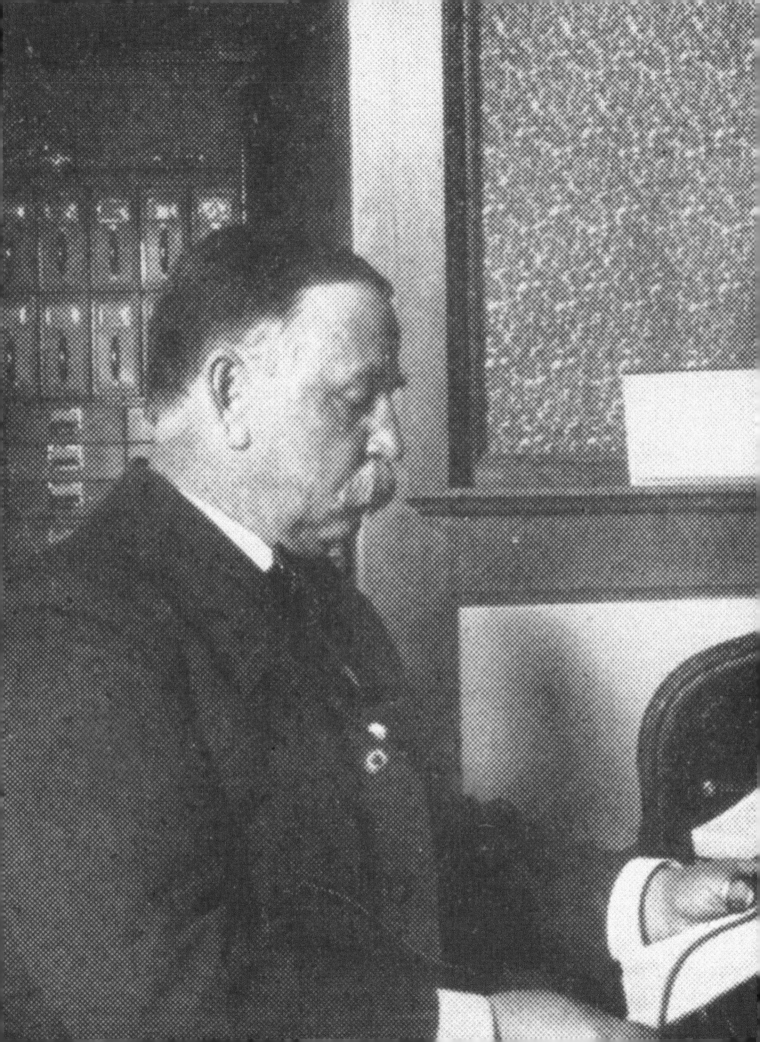

chapter three

THE ACADEMIC ENTERPRISE

No single individual had more impact on the new normal school than its first president, John Williston Cook (left). A native of New York, Cook moved with his family to Illinois at age seven to Kappa, a town near Bloomington. After graduating from high school, Cook tried farming and then railroading before taking up advanced studies at the newly created Illinois State Normal School in 1862. After three years, he graduated and left to teach in a rural school at Brimfield, west of Peoria. But his enthusiasm and brilliance left a mark on his professors, and when the town of Normal established a village school, the local board called Cook to be its principal—just one year after he had left. The following year he joined the Normal faculty and spent the next twenty-four years as a professor and then nine as president. While president, he came to know DeKalb newspaperman Clinton Rosette who had been appointed to the Board of Trustees by Governor Altgeld. Cook's excellent reputation for innovation and administration made him the clear first choice for the new Northern Illinois Normal School trustees. After a long negotiation, Cook agreed to take the job in the spring of 1899 and he started July first. Cook served Northern for twenty years and put his indelible mark on the school.

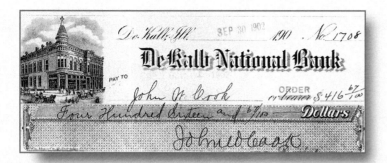

Fiscal controls were a bit looser a century ago: John W. Cook signed and endorsed his own paycheck. One point of interest is that Cook's salary, approximately four times that of his best-paid faculty when the school opened in 1899, remained the same throughout his twenty-year tenure as president. He never received a raise in pay.

The first month's payroll for the Northern Illinois State Normal School shows top professors on the staff earned about $1,000 a year. The NISNS board hired Cook at $5,000 per year and provided a house for him. The addendum to the bottom of this budget was a monthly honorarium for Newell D. Gilbert, the superintendent of the DeKalb Public Schools. The total payroll for Northern in its first year was about $20,000.

Automobiles were still a rarity when Northern opened its doors in 1899. With a view to the future, Altgeld Hall did have a carport built into the front facade to provide shelter from the elements. President Cook was the only member of the faculty or staff to own an auto in those first years, but soon other Northern faculty followed Cook's embrace of the newest transportation advance, and the flow through the turnaround in front of Altgeld increased.

One of the inducements Colonel Ellwood tossed into the package offered to the Illinois Legislature was the building of a house for the new president. A magnificent structure, this house still stands on Augusta Avenue and is only a short distance from Ellwood's own mansion that now serves as a DeKalb museum.

President's House, 1919

President Cook with Granddaughter Beatrice, 1905

President Cook set to building a faculty as soon as he agreed to terms with the new board. He brought several key members of the Illinois State Normal School faculty in Normal and hired others to complement this core. Charles McMurry (left) had earned his doctorate at Halle in Germany and was known for his pioneering methods in pedagogy, especially a movement called Herbartianism. He established the base for all of Northern's education departments and brought great credibility to the new school. In 1911, the trustees built a second building on the campus, a laboratory training school to complement local elementary schools. Named for Charles and Lida McMurry (Charles's sister-in-law and also a faculty member), the building still stands nearly one hundred years later. While McMurry was certainly the keystone of this new faculty, Cook's reputation and persuasive powers brought other top educators to the new school. Over half the faculty were women. The faculty not only regularly worked in the town schools, they also provided educational programs in the churches and factories. The Northern Illinois reported in June 1900 that "the last of the faculty lecture courses designed especially for the factory people of DeKalb was given by Mr. J. A. Switzer June 15 at 8:00 p.m. He had chosen as his subject 'The Roentgen Ray,' and when the hour arrived the hall was crowded."

From the beginning, the emphasis in teacher training was to combine practical experience with classroom recitation. President Cook hired Luther Hatch as first director of the training classrooms on campus, and Hatch then became superintendent of DeKalb schools in 1907. Students also went out into the DeKalb schools to put to the test what they had learned in the classroom. There was also in attendance a Critic Teacher to assess the student teaching performance and to make corrections in methods.

The Northern Illinois State Normal School

For the Preparation of Teachers for the Schools of Illinois

TUITION FREE
Complete Equipment

For Particulars
Address

N. I. S. N. S., De Kalb, Illinois

Cook brought Swen Parson with him from the Illinois State faculty and charged him with establishing the mathematics department. Parson remained head of mathematics until his death in 1935 and served the longest of any of the original faculty. Born in Sweden, Parson moved with his family to the United States as a teen. After a brief career teaching high school, Parson joined the faculty at ISNS in Normal and then moved to DeKalb with Cook in 1899. An avid athlete, Parson soon established himself as the faculty ace in both golf and tennis. He also served on the board of the DeKalb Public Library for forty-three years, chairing the board for all but the first two years. When he retired from teaching at the age of seventy-six, Parson undertook a six-month around-the-world trip. He died at the age of eighty-eight in 1949. His oil portrait hangs today in the reading room of the University Archives within Founders Library. Shortly after his death, Northern named the then new library in his honor. Today, Swen Parson Hall houses the College of Law, Information Technology Services, and several administrative units.

Since the idea of the normal school was to train students from the immediate rural area to become the teachers for that same area, there was no tuition when Northern first opened its doors. If one did not go on into teaching, however, the expectation was that the student would reimburse Northern for the cost of instruction. From the pages of the student newspaper we learn that the first tuition for attendance at the NISNS was received March 14 [1900]. "Miss Cora Sunderland has accepted a position as bookkeeper in the bank of her hometown, so she sent to the president the full tuition fee for the fall and winter terms of 1899 and 1900." In the class of 1903, only five students came from out of state, and over half came from just five counties: Kane (47), DeKalb (38), Cook (18), Ogle (14), and Whiteside (11). Women outnumbered men by more than five to one and the average age was twenty-two; there were also eleven students aged sixteen or seventeen and twenty-four students aged twenty-seven or older. A good number of these first students had already been teaching in the rural one-room schools of the northern Illinois region. Students could enroll in a one-, two-, or three-year course of studies depending on their preparation and their goals. Northern did require one full year in residence to earn a degree.

Biology Field Trip, 1900

Charles McMurry built a pedagogy curriculum, Edward C. Page established the history courses, Swen Parson created the mathematics and music departments, and Fred Lemar Charles set the foundations for the sciences in the new normal school. Charles's first loves were biology and botany, so he began by creating the labs and facilities necessary for teaching and experiments within the building. A Phi Beta Kappa scholar and published poet, Charles also enjoyed many sports. He organized and coached Northern's first tennis team and its baseball team (he played shortstop). He was second only to Swen Parson in the faculty tennis tourney. During the winter months, he convinced enough women to play basketball that Northern fielded a women's team before it had a men's team. During July and August, he regularly led faculty on long botanical field trips to the lower peninsula of Michigan. They camped out for weeks each summer. As if that was not enough to fill his schedule, Charles was a devoted family man with two young daughters. He also was the first adviser to the student newspaper, ran for DeKalb City Council in 1908 (and lost by four votes), was for many years the faculty adviser for the annual yearbook, did consulting for a Wisconsin rubber manufacturer (which took him to southern Mexico), regularly taught full loads in biology and botany, and enjoyed a reputation as a scholar in his field. In 1909, after ten productive years in DeKalb, the University of Illinois hired him away from Northern. He died at age thirty-eight, and his widow established a memorial at Northern to which many faculty, students, and alumni contributed. The Fred L. Charles Memorial Bench may still be seen just to the east of Swen Parson Hall in the pines.

Dry Valley Project, Antarctica 1972

Field trips in the natural sciences have become a staple of student life over the past century, and above, geology professor Ron Flemal led a class into the Black Hills of South Dakota on a summer expedition in 1983. By then, the Northern Geology Department had established itself nationally and was a major partner in Antarctic research. Northern's field research began with the Dry Valley Drilling Project in 1973, a collaborative effort with organizations in Japan, New Zealand, and the United States. With substantial support from the National Science Foundation's Polar Programs, the project sought "to study the paleontological evolution of marine polar life and to establish a precise record of the periodicity of glacial pulsation, volcanic eruptions, magnetic reversals, and climate variations." Professor Lyle McGinnis, coordinator of the DVDP in the 1970s, said the lowest temperature he had recorded while working there was minus seventy degrees Fahrenheit. "You don't think about fear or death," McGinnis remembered, but "you never go anywhere with just one person or one vehicle." Graduate student Tim Fasnacht recalled that "you take that first step off the plane into cold clean air and you can't speak. . . .You see ice everywhere with the snowy Transantarctic Mountains jutting into the distant skyline." Dry Valley is a 4,000-square-mile area free of snow and still holding secrets that, if exposed, may help to explain the history of climate on our planet. Fred Charles would be dazzled by where his intrepid beginnings in 1899 have led for Northern scientists. The records of the early years of the Dry Valley project including some photographs and diaries now reside in the University Archives.

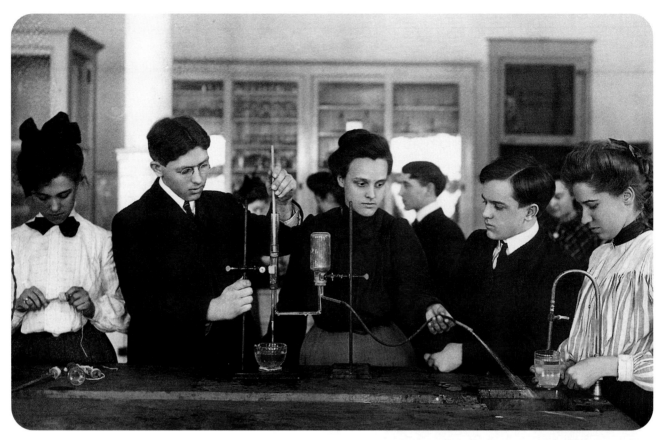

From the beginning, Northern's science faculty has also made a home and a name for itself in the laboratory. When classes began in the fall of 1899, the labs were not ready nor had the equipment arrived. "Temporary tables have been put in to accommodate the classes until later when we will have fuller equipment," the student newspaper reported. Soon, sixteen compound microscopes had arrived as well as aquaria of plant and animal life and a good supply of working materials including clams, crayfish, and grasshoppers. The following year on March 12 came the first major accident in the chemistry lab when "a violent explosion burned Mr. Wiltse's right hand. The phosphorous kept burning for a while," according to a report in the Northern Illinois, "but he is healing slowly now." The photograph above, from a 1900 lantern slide, is titled "Making a Force Pump."

In the biological sciences, NIU faculty became part of national efforts to advance knowledge in virtually every field. Geneticist Sidney Mittler (right), Northern legend holds, had the largest collection of fruit flies in the country at one point in time. Mittler came to NIU in 1960 after a fifteen-year career in both the academic and corporate research worlds. He spent the remainder of his career at NIU and published over one hundred scholarly articles. Mittler's research specialized in radiation and chemical mutagenesis. His work for the U.S. Army in the 1970s irradiating food pioneered that field of research. Much of his later career research focused on cancer, and it was that disease that took his life in 1988. While Mittler worked in genetics, his colleagues worked in AIDS research, hematology, immunology, and epidemiology as they sought answers to some of the most complex and difficult problems facing an overpopulated world.

The computer and telecommunications advances of the 1970s and 1980s offered researchers instant access to colleagues and resources around the world. Successful applications to national agencies and foundations brought in the revenue necessary to move forward in the high technology world of the eighties and nineties. The establishment of the Plant Molecular Biology Research Center in 1989 was one example of nearly a dozen centers created to further research and public service.

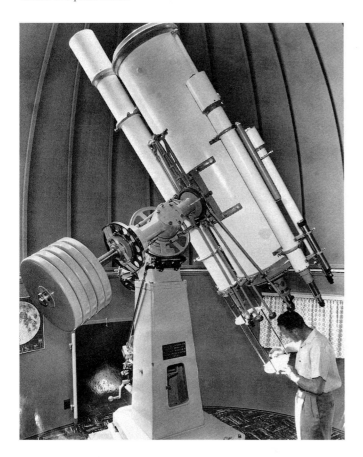

While most of the physical scientists focused their attention on problems here on earth, with the construction of Davis Hall in the 1940s, a window to the universe also became part of teaching and research at Northern. As the home of earth sciences, Davis Hall offered a view of the heavens through its rooftop observatory. Here, too, the university upgraded its scientific equipment, installing a sixteen-inch Cassegrain Newtonian reflector telescope in the spring of 1965. Built by the Michimuri Company in Kyoto, Japan, the telescope cost $15,000 to purchase and install. Generations of NIU students have had their first close look at the solar system through the view afforded by the Davis Hall Observatory. Physics professors Ralph Benbow and David Hedin led an effort to upgrade the observatory in 2000 and secured the funding required. The observatory serves as a teaching aid for physics and geology courses and is open for public tours one night a week. Today, Davis Hall is still the home for the geography, geology, and meteorology programs and houses a large map library and cartographic laboratory.

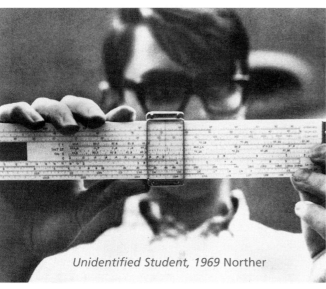

Unidentified Student, 1969 Norther

The digital computer revolution of the last quarter of the twentieth century brought the greatest changes in scientific research and teaching in the twentieth century. Through the 1950s and into the 1960s, both teachers and students relied on mechanical calculating machines and the ever-present slide rule for assisting with the basic math necessary for physical science. For students before 1970, the slide rule was the sine qua non for all classes in physics and chemistry. In mathematics, chemistry, physics, and engineering, the arrival of ever cheaper and more effective digital computing would bring advances in research. Beginning in the 1960s, computer science as a field in its own right began to develop, usually within the mathematics department as was the case at NIU.

IBM Digital
Computer at
NIU, 1963

Scientists created digital computers during World War II, working on a foundation
first laid in the nineteenth century by Charles Babbage's calculating machines.
Progress was painstakingly slow until transistors and, eventually, integrated circuitry
revolutionized microelectronics. Northern leased its first computer from IBM, and
the agreement brought IBM technicians to campus in 1962 to teach faculty and
staff how to use it. Extremely large and slow by later standards, the early computers
required a lot of space that was carefully controlled for internal environment. The
entire campus shared one computer. In 1967, Northern upgraded to the legendary
IBM 360 and never looked back.

Northern's first personal computer arrived in July of 1978, a Commodore PET
with a cassette tape drive and featuring 4K RAM, a seven-inch monochrome
CRT, and a five-by-seven-inch keyboard. Academic Computer Services purchased
the unit for $711, and it now resides within the University Archives, complete with
the heavy steel cable that was fastened to the wall to prevent "borrowing." The
University Archives also holds the first personal computer purchased by the library
in 1983 for $64.95 from Kmart. That was a Times Sinclair 1000 model and
featured 16K RAM, connections to a full-size television CRT, and a full-size
keyboard. Thus, the price of a personal computer had dropped in the first five years
by ninety percent while the capacity for processing data had increased 400 percent.
That extraordinary beginning of the upward curve of more and more performance
for lower and lower price continued for the next thirty years and changed life on
the campus in every way.

While digital computers revolutionized the physical sciences, the social sciences at Northern, too, began a major process of change. No one more symbolized the change from bucolic teacher's college to the world of the modern research university than Professor Earl W. Hayter (left with his papers, 1979). Hayter had earned his doctorate at Northwestern University in the middle of the Great Depression and came to Northern on a temporary, one-year contract in 1936. Over the next thirty years, he would lead the way to a new era in scholarship and teaching as he presided over the end of the old social sciences department. The social sciences and humanities, too, began in the 1960s to specialize and sought to bring advanced research into classroom teaching. Professor Hayter, a nationally known authority in agricultural history, recruited scholars with doctoral degrees and an interest in research for the newly created history department. Northern's governing board had approved the first master's degrees in education in 1951 and within a decade established the first doctoral degree programs in English, history, education, and business education. Hayter remained on the history faculty until he retired from active teaching in 1969. He then took five years to write the history of Northern, Education in Transition, to commemorate the celebration of NIU's seventy-fifth anniversary.

At the end of his academic career, Hayter mused that humankind "continuously searches and explores for meaning even to the end of life, recognizing, however, that about all that is real in this quest for understanding is the tremendous sense of adventure you will experience along the way." Earl W. Hayter's personal adventure ended in DeKalb June 8, 1994, at the age of ninety-three. His papers and his autobiography now reside in the University Archives that he helped to establish in 1964.

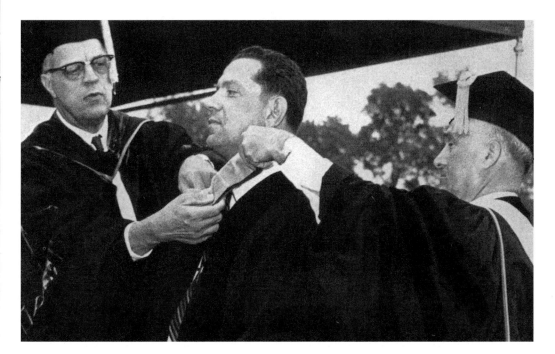

Herbert J. Bergstein earned the first doctoral degree at Northern in business education in 1964. In this photo, Graduate School Dean Robert L. Thistlewaite (left) and Vice President Francis R. Geigle (right) fasten the doctoral hood and confer the degree.

Northern's nationally recognized School of Music also traces its foundation to an extraordinary professor, Charles Elliot Fouser (above). Fouser, who arrived on campus in 1931, had taken his graduate degrees at Northwestern University and the Cincinnati Conservatory of Music. Northern's administration persuaded him to leave the University of Illinois to come to DeKalb to build a broad and strong program. In just fifteen years, Fouser had laid the foundation for what would become one of the university's largest and most acclaimed academic programs. Known for his music compositions, his organ playing, and his classroom teaching, Fouser was the prototype of the faculty that would, in the era of the university, combine research, teaching, and public service. Symphonies still play his best-known composition, The Prairie Symphony, in concert halls around the country. Among his many activities, Fouser was organist and music director at the First United Methodist Church in DeKalb where he wrote original pieces for both organ and chorus and directed the choir. Like many professors of the period, he lived in a home just east of the campus. His home was conveniently about halfway between the campus and the church. He installed an organ in his home and was seated at that organ working on a composition titled The Beatitudes on the evening of October 14, 1946. There, still seated at his organ, he died of a sudden and massive heart attack at the age of fifty-five. His legacy to Northern is recounted on a bronze plaque in the Music Library that is named in his honor. The choir of the Methodist Church performed The Beatitudes for the first time at his funeral service.

The growth of the School of Music came with the change to university status in 1957 and the establishment of degree programs in music including graduate degrees. In the last half of the twentieth century, student and faculty performance groups became NIU's ambassadors to the world. Three groups stood out in bringing the excellence of music to the national and international stage: the Vermeer Quartet, the NIU Jazz Band, and the Steel Drum Band.

Northern's resident faculty string quartet, the Vermeer, celebrated its twenty-fifth anniversary in 1994. Just two years later, the group's recording of Haydn's Seven Last Words of Christ received a nomination for a Grammy Award. The Vermeer annually tours Europe, plays to sellout crowds at American venues, and spends part of each summer in Maine to recharge the musical batteries. Lead violinist Schmuel Ashkenasi (far left) has been with the group since its inception. Its European tours have brought many graduate students to Northern to study with members of the group. The image here is from 1971.

Ron Modell established a jazz band when he came to NIU and, over two decades, nurtured it to national prominence. The NIU Jazz Band won numerous Down Beat magazine awards, toured Europe to enthusiastic audiences, cut several compact disks, and became one of Northern's crown jewels. Modell retired in 1998, and his first retirement gig was a national tour with the band backing pop star Phil Collins. Here, Modell is seen in his role as teacher with student Angel Rodriguez in a 1993 photo.

The third jewel in the crown of the NIU School of Music is the Steel Drum Band. Created by Professor Allan O'Connor, this band really took off in popularity and performance when professional drum builder Cliff Alexis agreed to leave Trinidad to work in DeKalb at Northern. The band would eventually tour the world and make a reputation for itself matched by few groups on the national collegiate music scene.

NIU Steel Drum Band, 1976, at the Music Building

NIU Steel Drum Band in Taiwan, the Asian Tour, 1992

Today, the School of Music's traveling ensembles often recruit graduate students to study at Northern, many of them from Europe and Asia. International students first arrived on the campus in 1904 from the Philippines. The first six arrived in DeKalb as a part of a much larger group that arrived in California sponsored by the Philippine government. After completing college preparatory work in California secondary schools, these students moved on to various colleges around the United States for further training. Some of those who wanted to become teachers came to Northern through the efforts of President Cook. A total of eleven foreign students came between 1904 and 1907. Students from the Philippines continued to come to Northern and still do today, one hundred years later. The entire Southeast Asian region eventually became one of the primary sources for Northern's international student population. These first students all studied pedagogy and went on to become schoolteachers and administrators. The trickle of incoming international students became a steady flow beginning in 1970, and in 2000, Northern enrolled over 1,200 foreign students with India (307), China (141), and Korea (82) leading the list of countries sending students. Forty-five came from the Philippines.

History professor J. Norman Parmer and political science professor Daniel Wit worked hard to bring a Peace Corps training program to Northern when President Kennedy first established that initiative. Parmer was the first history department chair after the old social sciences unit split up. Parmer and Wit did secure a program to train Peace Corps workers for Southeast Asia in 1961. Successful negotiations between R. Sargent Shriver Jr. and Malayan Prime Minister Tengku Abdul Rahman brought the first class of trainees to DeKalb. The group of volunteers arrived at NIU October 14, 1961. In this picture, volunteers J. Patrick White (second from left) and J. Norman Parmer (far right), history professors, greet Peter Kramer (left) and Sadie Stout (third from left) as they check in at the Rice Hotel in downtown DeKalb. The Rice Hotel itself thus began a long, convoluted history with the university that would culminate in NIU owning the facility after a complete rehabilitation in the 1980s.

Peace Corps Training Dance Masks

As the Peace Corps Training Program took shape with its focus on the Southeast Asian countries of Malaysia, the Philippines, and Thailand, Professors Parmer and M. Ladd Thomas enlisted President Holmes's support for a Southeast Asian Studies Center. Both Parmer and Thomas had extensive field experience in Southeast Asia, and the region was seen as critical to continued American security in the effort to curb the growth of Communism. The SEA Center would be an academic study area and would be supported by a significant collection of materials within the library. In the decades since its creation in 1960, the NIU Southeast Asian Studies Center and program has become one of the premier programs in the country. The Donn Hart Collection within the University Libraries supports the center's graduate research efforts. The Peace Corps program came under its administrative aegis in 1963.

While the Peace Corps Training Program closed, the SEA Center continued to grow and thrive. The Burma Studies Group of the Association for Asian Studies established the Center for Burma Studies on the NIU campus in 1986. A natural outgrowth of the Southeast Asian Studies Center, the Burma Center also strengthened the university's museum holdings with a Burma Gallery, and the library worked to strengthen its holdings on Burmese life and history. Professor Catherine Raymond is the current director of the center that is part of the graduate programs at NIU and affiliated with the Burma Studies Foundation. The Burma Gallery, part of the NIU Art Museum, holds a strong collection of Burmese art and artifacts. In this photograph, Buddhist monk U Pannadipa performs a dedication ceremony for the new center in 1987.

The Southeast Asian Center and the Center for Burma Studies were just two of many academic centers created in the last thirty years at Northern. One of the effects of the cultural revolution of the sixties on American campuses was the establishment of cross-disciplinary research and public service interests. The traditional academic model of college and department did not serve well, and campuses across the country began to create centers. At Northern, the SEA Center and the Center for Burma Studies were joined by the Center for Black Studies, the Center for Latino Studies, the Women's Studies Center, the Social Science Research Institute, the Local Government Studies Center, the Regional History Center, and the Plant Molecular Biology Center.

DeKalb's Rice Hotel, which welcomed the Peace Corps trainees in the 1960s, would become the Social Science Research Institute in the 1980s. The Institute attracted both public and private grants and contracts to fund, in part, the projects carried out under its umbrella, and it offered a place for faculty and graduate students to work in advanced research and public policy.

The College of Liberal Arts and Sciences created the Office for Social Science Research on August 1, 1980, and this became the SSRI in 1982 when the Board of Regents integrated several existing programs and research areas into a single administrative structure. The goal was to develop policy and research services that address the public priorities of the state and the nation and to foster original research that would lead to new knowledge in the social sciences. Through a long, ten-year lease-purchase process, the university worked with a private developer to rehabilitate completely the old hotel, and NIU now owns the facility, which is located near the center of downtown DeKalb. Over the years, the SSRI has been the source for a steady stream of newsletters, monographs, occasional bulletins, bibliographies, research papers, and cartographic studies. Components of the Institute have changed through the years, and currently there are five centers under its umbrella: the American Farmland Trust Center for Agriculture in the Environment, the Center for Governmental Studies, the National Social Norms Resource Center, the Office for Social Policy Research, and the Public Opinion Lab. The university named the facility for William R. Monat in 2005.

Two primary issues generated new directions in research in the humanities and social sciences from the 1960s forward: race and gender. NIU created three distinct centers and programs to encourage and facilitate work in the areas of race and gender. The Women's Studies Program had a number of homes following its creation in 1976, as did University Resources for Women since its beginning in 1979. The URW eventually settled into what was known as the Wirtz House on Normal Road at the center of the campus in the 1980s. Soon, however, campus renewal brought the Martin Luther King Jr. Commons to the area between the library and the student center. This project also required razing the Wirtz House. Those involved in the University Resources for Women advocated for a place that would continue the warm, homey feel of the old Wirtz House yet keep them close to the middle of campus. The Arndt House at the corner of Lincoln Highway and Normal Road—just a

block south of the Wirtz location—proved to be just what was needed. Renovations totaling $237,000 expanded and renewed the 1905 brick structure to a total of 6,000 square feet. In November 1990, the new Center opened for business. NIU created the Presidential Commission on the Status of Women, which advises the administration on women's issues campuswide as a complement to the academic program and the resources center.

Immediately to the west of the Women's Center on Lincoln Highway, Northern demolished several single-family residences it had acquired to construct a new home for the Center for Black Studies and the Black Studies Program. After breaking ground for the project April 18, 1993, construction proceeded rapidly, and the 4,000-square-foot building was already open for use in August of 1993. In addition to housing the academic Black Studies Program, the Center is a social focus and home away from home for many of Northern's African American students. The Center offers a home also for the academic minor in Black Studies, an interdisciplinary venture involving the social sciences and

humanities. Through mentoring programs, speakers, workshops, and cultural events, the Center provides a nurturing environment for African American students. One of the Center's most successful annual events has been the African American Leadership Conference held each spring on the NIU campus.

TV Talk Show Hostess Bertice Berry, 1998

Harvard's Cornell West, 1998

Issues of gender and race often overlap, and when the Center for Black Studies initiated an annual African American Leadership Conference in 1995, it brought people such as Harvard University's Cornell West and talk show hostess Bertice Berry to campus to speak. This tradition at Northern goes back over thirty years to appearances by such notables as Angela Davis, Julian Bond, Alex Haley, Jesse Jackson, and Bill Cosby in the 1960s.

Center for Latino and Latin American Affairs

Like other centers that NIU created in the 1970s, the Center for Latino and Latin American Affairs first found quarters in one of the many houses purchased on the periphery of the campus, in this case on Garden Road across from Anderson Hall.

Danca Quenta, 1997

The NIU Administration created a complementary unit, University Resources for Latinos, to provide encouragement and support for Latino and Latina students coming to study on campus and to bring diversity to the campus. Latin music, dance, and theater became part of the campus culture in the 1990s. The URL program, for many years, made its home in the old Oderkirk House on Annie Glidden Road, all the way across the campus from the Latino Studies Center.

After settling into the Garden Road building, it became apparent that the rapid growth in the number of students and programs required newer, larger quarters. Northern completed work on a new facility at the Garden Road location that could bring both programs together and give them a quality, permanent home. The Center's opening coincided with the twenty-fifth anniversary of the creation of the minor in Latino Studies, an interdisciplinary program that drew on several departments within the College of Liberal Arts and Sciences.

Yet another center NIU created in the 1970s, the Regional History Center, brought together in balance the three-fold mission of the modern public university: research, teaching, and public service. The Center used the University Archives as its core and expanded into the collection and preservation of historical records from the university's eighteen-county northern Illinois service area. Through a contract with the Illinois State Archives, the Regional History Center collects and makes available for research local government records with historical value. Thus naturalization, education, land, court, and census records dating back to the first half of the nineteenth century are now found in the Center's holdings. The Illinois State Archives has invested over half a million dollars in the collection and continues to employ two full-time graduate assistants annually.

Regional History Center staff also collected historical records from family farms, churches, grain elevators, civic organizations, politicians, small businesses, and social organizations to complement the story told in the local government records. After a quarter-century, the Center's 600 collections cover over 7,000 feet of shelving and offer researchers the primary sources to tell the region's history. The photographs in this book have come from the nearly 700,000 images held in the collections.

The view above is from the corner of Main Street (Lincoln Highway) and Seventh Street looking to the west. This photograph is from the Center's Embree Collection, which holds over ten thousand photographs from DeKalb dating from 1892 to 1965. A second large section of the Embree Collection depicts railroading in the first half of the twentieth century; there are over forty thousand images in the railroad collection.

Thousands of researchers visit the Center each year; over half have no affiliation with NIU. Many students and classes also come in to do research, and the Center has employed nearly one hundred graduate interns over the years to train them on the job in public history. The Center staff also teaches research methods in primary historical sources and works with local historical societies and museums throughout the northern Illinois region.

The image here is also from the Embree Collection and shows Teddy Roosevelt speaking on Republican Charles Evans Hughes's whistle stop tour in DeKalb during the 1916 Presidential Campaign. It was Roosevelt's second speaking appearance in DeKalb as he had spoken sixteen years earlier in his own bid for the presidency. Roosevelt's train had rolled in from Dixon just after noon and was met by a large crowd, a band, and 115 mounted former members of his Spanish-American War Rough Riders. A short parade took Roosevelt, the band, and the crowd down Main Street to a small wooded area just southwest of the lagoon. New York Senator Mark Hanna introduced Teddy to the crowd, and he began his standard stump speech attacking the Democrats. The crowd had difficulty hearing him as the campaign trail had severely damaged his speaking voice. After the speech, Roosevelt and his entourage retired to the Ellwood House for refreshments before boarding the campaign trail for Belvidere at mid-afternoon. To commemorate the event, townspeople erected a stone marker in the woods that stood until torn down in March 1966.

"The gateman rang his bell and Fireman Smith threw on the brakes and the machine skidded upon the track stopping right in the way of the train. . . . When the engineer saw that he could not stop the train, he probably threw the throttle wide open and hit the truck hard enough to clear it from the tracks. The train must have been going at the rate of about 50 miles an hour when it crossed the bridge, and there was no chance for the engineer to stop after the truck appeared." That was the story in a nutshell as reported by the DeKalb Daily Chronicle June 17, 1913. Few people knew how to drive automobiles and, when DeKalb bought its first mechanized fire truck in the fall of 1912, all the firemen needed to be trained to drive the new vehicle. Unfortunately, fireman L. L. Smith's first training trip was his last. The photo is one of many held by the Center that has been used by researchers in exhibits, research papers, and publications.

Moving Day,
December 8, 1952

At the heart of the academic enterprise is the library, the place that acquires, preserves, and transmits knowledge. That is as true today as it was in 1899 when Northern opened its doors. The format may have expanded to include electronic databases, microforms, and cartographic records, but the role is the same and it is to support the students and faculty in their quest to learn and teach. The Haish Library located in Altgeld Hall served well for the first fifty years, but a growing institution demanded new and much larger quarters by the late 1940s.

When the Swen Franklin Parson Library opened in 1952, Northern decided to use a student and faculty brigade to move the materials from the old Haish Library on the second floor of Altgeld to the new building next door. In a well-choreographed snake dance, hundreds of students, faculty, and staff kept the human conveyer moving throughout the day. President Holmes himself led with the first armload of books. The students followed in tight procession. The Dames Club set up refreshment stands with free donuts and coffee for the volunteers. In one day, this makeshift army moved 83,000 books weighing 85 tons, and they downed 110 gallons of coffee and 250 dozen donuts in the process. That worked out to one donut for every twenty-eight books moved, a bargain for the taxpayers.

The crown jewel added to the Northern campus in the 1950s was the Swen Franklin Parson Library. Set halfway between Adams Hall on the north and Davis Hall on the south, the library replaced Altgeld Hall as the focus of campus life for students. Northern had long outgrown the Haish Library on the second floor of Altgeld Hall. With the postwar enrollment growth, a new library became the top priority, and trustees broke ground in December of 1949. The new library's Gothic architectural style, leaded glass windows, and soaring vaulted entrance greeted generations of Northern students with an air akin to the great university libraries of Europe. It matched in style and material both Adams and Davis Halls that preceded it on the Normal Road boundary of the campus. A pair of matching card catalogs opposed the circulation desk and provided access to the 100,000 volumes held by 1955. Within the library, such treasures as an art gallery, a music room, and a state-of-the-art lecture hall provided students with new opportunities to learn within the library building. Demands for more space created the north and south wing additions of the 1960s. Today, the building serves as the home of the NIU College of Law and also for several administrative offices in the north wing.

The Haish Library served Northern for fifty years, but the Parson Library had only half that life; by the 1970s, construction was underway to replace it with Founders Memorial Library. Designed by the firm of Hellmuth, Obata, and Kassabaum, the building cost $13.5 million for approximately 300,000 square feet. Construction took just under four years, and in January 1977, the new library opened to students and faculty. As its twenty-fifth anniversary arrived in 2002, a $4 million expansion opened the basement of the building for compact shelving storage of low-use items. By then, the library held 1.8 million print volumes, over a million microforms, and thousands of serial runs. In addition to all this material, Founders Library now has over 300 computers providing both staff and students access to bibliographic information, the Internet, more than one hundred electronic databases, and electronic reserves for classes. Beyond these traditional functions, the library is also the home for three smart classrooms, a large student computer lab, and the Lincoln Digital Library Project. A student from 1899 would, no doubt, be dazzled by what has happened in the century since the first library opened in Altgeld. In 2004, the library passed the 2 million mark in total volumes held.

Chosen carefully
One of a thousand designs
What were they thinking?

Perhaps NIU alumni better remember nothing more than the carpeting on the main floor of the library. A devilishly bright yellow and black stripe, the carpet can give one the woozies if stared at long enough. The carpet proved extraordinarily durable and, twenty-five years after its installation, is still in excellent shape for new generations of students to enjoy. Who picked it out? You would have to visit the NIU Archives to find the answer to that question. The Library's Rare Books Department solicited poems describing the carpet in a 2003 contest. Anthropology graduate student Sarah E. Koepke wrote the winning entry, a "carpet haiku" (above right). In 2005 Library Dean Arthur P. Young secured the funds to replace the carpet.

chapter four

ATHLETICS

From the beginning, football has been the cornerstone of intercollegiate athletics at Northern. With only twenty-five men in the first class, fielding a football team posed some problems. Nonetheless, Northern won its first game on November 10, 1899, over DeKalb High School 16 to 10. Since Northern was only a two-year school and had few men in attendance, most games in the early years were played against area high schools and factory teams. This particular flier (top of next page) announced the game would take place after New York Governor Theodore Roosevelt's speech. Roosevelt was campaigning for the presidency at the time and spoke in what is now the Montgomery Arboretum, just several hundred yards south of the football field in 1900. It was Roosevelt who would later initiate the first major national investigation of college football because of the number of players who were killed or seriously injured in the sport.

Football Practice, 1901

Baseball and football became the foundation team sports at Northern for men. With no full-time coaches in the early years, faculty did double duty. Mathematics professor Swen Parson even filled in as a shortstop on the first baseball teams. Parson also served as the first golf coach, and his colleague, biology professor Fred Charles, as the first baseball coach. William Wirtz, shown here (right) at a baseball practice, doubled as Northern's first athletic director. Baseball continued as the primary spring sport until the NIU Athletic Board dropped it in 1982. The Board reversed its decision after nearly ten years, and in 1991, baseball once again heralded the arrival of spring on the Northern campus. The photo above shows biology professor/baseball coach Fred Charles with the 1902 team.

The attrition of male students during World War I and the growth of public interest in collegiate athletics led President J. Stanley Brown to embrace sports as a way to bring men to the campus and positive publicity to the school. Brown hired William Muir (left) as the football coach in 1923, and Muir later also coached the basketball team. Muir was the first trained coach who was a full-time professional. The effort to upgrade men's sports did bring a substantial increase in male enrollment, but the venture turned sour when Muir used nonstudents and ineligible players to build a winning record. Worse, an internal investigation implicated President Brown, himself, in the win-at-all-costs deceptions. The ensuing public imbroglio brought Muir's resignation and sullied Brown's public image.

"THE NORMAL GIRL AT DEKALB, ILL."

Well I guess!
Well I guess!
N. I. S. N. S.
Yes! Yes!

Professor Fred Charles created Northern's first official cheer in a Pep Assembly in September 1899. "Well, I guess! Well, I guess! . . . N. I. S. N. S. . . . Yes!! Yessss!!" The students voted yellow and white their official school colors; the athletic booster club successfully lobbied for the athletic colors of cardinal and black in 1906. The postcard shown here was printed in color with a pennant of yellow background and white lettering. From the beginning, women were actively involved in all aspects of life outside the classroom, including athletics. "Three cheers and a tiger for our girls' basketball team! They bravely carry off the laurel from the team of Wheaton. The gym was packed and enthusiasm reached its zenith. Finest game ever played in the gym. Score of 13 to 40," the 1900 Norther reported.

Women began playing intramural basketball in the fall of 1899, and Professor Charles quickly organized a team that could represent Northern against other normal schools, small colleges, and area high schools. Basketball had only been invented in 1892 and was still a new sport to most people in 1899, but Northern had both women's and men's teams from the first year forward. It only took four years before the inevitable: a group of athletic enthusiasts from outside the school organized to support Northern's teams. To bring its athletic relations with the school to a business and perhaps permanent basis, the alumni met and organized the Alumni Athletic Association. The group elected mathematics professor Swen Parson its treasurer and faculty liaison and then promptly raised the $300 necessary to hire a coach. Within two years, the AAA also had succeeded in getting Northern to adopt cardinal and black as the school athletic colors. In addition to the traditional interscholastic sports teams, there were a number of club and intramural sports, including a golf club and a tennis association. Inside the gymnasium, one could find a complete array of gymnastics equipment, a bowling alley, and a basketball court with lines for women's softball.

Women first played with a very large and soft ball in the gym, but soon they moved outside and adopted the smaller harder ball we know today. Interscholastic play then began in 1917 for what was known as Playground Ball. By the end of the twentieth century, women's intercollegiate softball had become a major sport nationwide and an Olympic sport as well. Today's players not only enjoy athletic scholarship support, they travel south for early spring training, have full-time coaches and trainers, and play on a field designed and maintained just for their sport. Mary Bell Field is named for the coach who set the foundation for modern intercollegiate softball at Northern. Bell, softball coach from 1959 through 1974, is a charter member of the NIU Athletic Hall of Fame.

NIU Yearbook, 1917

In the 1970s under Coach Bell, the women's softball team played its games on a field just east of Anderson Hall as seen at top. Spectators brought lawn chairs, there was no backstop, and groundskeepers chalked the lines in over the grass. When Northern's Athletic Board cut men's baseball in 1982, the women moved to McKinzie Field just northwest of Huskie Stadium and continued to play there until the opening of Mary Bell Field (bottom photo) east of Huskie Stadium in 1992. McKinzie Field once again became the home for the men's baseball team when Northern reinstated the sport in 1991.

Although intercollegiate basketball was the only sport in which women competed with other schools in the early decades, club and intramural sports such as golf, tennis, field hockey, and softball gained in popularity. Some of these eventually also became intercollegiate sports. The many physical training classes offered in the curriculum included archery, bowling, swimming, and track. The 1920s, often called the golden age of sport in America, generated extraordinary interest in all types of athletic activities on the campus. Field hockey remained an important sport for women at Northern through the 1980s before it died out across the country as interest in other sports grew. The field hockey team played on fields lined out just to the north of Anderson Hall and on the Huskie Stadium Astroturf until the Athletic Board dropped that sport in 1992.

Elmer "Curly" Rich, 1927

Peg Wilson, 1927

With all the new athletic activities in the 1920s came the demand for better organized cheering sections at the games and meets. In the spring of 1927, the Northern Illinois announced there would be "try outs for cheerleaders, not only boys but girls as well. A need for more than one cheerleader has long been felt." So the Varsity Club offered an official sweater as inducement and the Women's Athletic Association matched it for a female cheerleader. Elmer "Curly" Rich and Peg Wilson won the competition and became the first official Northern cheerleaders in the fall of 1927. For seventy-five years, cheerleaders have led NIU students and fans in support of their teams joined in later decades by the band, pom pom squads, and the NIU Silverettes.

Cheerleader Carole Engbrecht, 1961

Victor E. Huskie, 1996 Edition

One of the Homecoming activities popular in the middle decades of the twentieth century was the annual bonfire to inspire the students and build spirit for the weekend. Bonfires, parades, and formal dances surrounded the centerpiece, the Saturday afternoon football game. One thing remained constant in the first one hundred years of Huskie athletics, and that is the support of the fans: fan is simply the short form of fanatic.

There have been many iterations of the traditional NIU mascot, both the human and the canine variety. This is the symbol by which Northern is known across the country though NIU teams have had several different monikers over the years. For more information on mascots, team names, cheers, athletic colors, logos, and songs see "A Northern Almanac" on page 200.

Football has always gotten the lion's share of interest in intercollegiate athletics, and, by most accounts, DeKalb native Reino Nori (above) was the best of the best in the first half-century of Northern football. The "Flying Finn" played four years, led the conference in scoring in 1935, and was a unanimous choice for all-conference halfback. Nori also excelled in other sports; he had already earned seven varsity letters by the end of his sophomore year. By the time he graduated he had earned seventeen letters, an all-time record. He led the 1935 basketball team in scoring, played third base in the spring, and managed to broad jump 22' 6" in the conference track meet. In 1936, Nori won the conference basketball scoring title, and coaches named him the league's most valuable player. Here he is seen running the ball in a 1934 practice. After graduating, he played in the Chicago Tribune All-Star Game and then professionally with the Chicago Bears, the Detroit Lions, and the Brooklyn Dodgers. In the winters, he came back to his alma mater to coach the wrestling team. An extraordinary man, Nori died at age seventy-five in his hometown of DeKalb on October 8, 1988.

The Great Depression also saw the first African American athletes competing for Northern. Elzie Cooper (right), from nearby Rochelle, played both football and basketball from 1933 to 1937 when he became an assistant football coach. Northern's teams during this period were known as the Profs—Huskies did not become the name until 1940—and it was during Cooper's first year on campus that A. Neil Annas published his "Loyalty Song" and "Alma Mater." The 1920s may have been the golden age in American sports, but at Northern, it would be the thirties that would become the transformation of sport in scope and successes.

An Aurora native, Chet Davis earned twelve varsity letters, four each in football, basketball, and track. Like Reino Nori before him, Davis earned all-conference quarterback honors as a sophomore, won several conference championships, and was a legend among the local sports fans. When Davis finished his football career on his twenty-first birthday, his friends threw a huge party at the Lincoln Inn the night of the victory over Illinois State. In the four conference games that year, Northern outscored its opponents by a combined score of 74–0. On May 26, 1939, Chet Davis closed his athletic career at the Little Nineteen Conference track meet in Macomb where he led Northern to a conference championship and set a conference scoring record. Davis placed second in the 100- and 220-yard dashes, second in the broad jump, and fourth in the high jump.

From 1899, tennis had been an intramural sport for both students and faculty, but under George Terwilliger, Northern fielded its first intercollegiate tennis team in 1929 (pictured below). Golf, tennis, track, and other minor sports also flourished in the thirties. None, of course, enjoyed scholarship support, full-time coaches, or travel budgets.

Smith on the Glidden Track, 1948

Elected Senior Class President for 1948–1949, Ernest C. "Bumpy" Smith was yet another sign of the new order. A World War II Navy veteran, Smith had first come to campus in 1942 before leaving for war service. He returned to DeKalb in 1946. Smith was one of those extraordinary people who did it all. He was secretary of Alpha Phi Omega, president of the Social Science Club, and a member of the Philosophy Club. Smith completed a double major in psychology and social science, ran track for four years, and enjoyed a nonstop social life on the side. It was also Smith who was refused service at the Log Cabin Restaurant, which led to the first public civil rights protests in DeKalb. Smith now resides in a Detroit suburb after a long and successful career as a teacher. Track coach Carl Appell helped to find Smith part-time employment, and he lived, at first, in temporary barracks housing brought to the NIU campus from Camp McCoy in Wisconsin. "The first two years [after the war] everybody on the track team but one guy was a veteran," according to Smith. "That's how predominant veterans were at that stage."

One of Bumpy Smith's track teammates was fellow Navy veteran, Tarver "Cy" Perkins (at left). Perkins first came to Northern in 1940 and was conference champion in the 880 for three years before enlisting in the Navy in 1943. He returned to Northern in the fall of 1946 to finish his education and went on a European tour with the American AAU team in the summer of 1947. On that tour, he set an American record for the half-mile in Bislet Stadium in Oslo, one minute fifty seconds. Perkins, a Native American of Cherokee descent, came to Northern after Carl Appell recruited him fresh from high school in Cleveland, Ohio. Perkins now lives in Geneseo, Illinois, and continues to pursue his career in transportation management.

When asked about his extraordinary accomplishments in running track, Perkins is quick to credit the hard-nosed coach who recruited him. He would play handball for as much as two hours over a long lunch with his coach, but then, "I can remember Carl saying as he left the handball court, 'Don't let that keep you from running five miles tonight.'" So day after day in the winter cold, they would run the miles along Annie Glidden Road, then over to First Street, back into town. At the end of the course, he would turn at the Ellwood House, and then "whatever I had left, I'd open up and stride out as long as I could. Come down the hill, across the bridge, and over into the parking lot, and there was Still Gym." All that each day through the cold and the snow of a DeKalb winter.

The only NIU student to win an Olympic gold medal, Ken Henry (left), won the 400-meter speed skating title for the United States in Bislet Stadium, Oslo, Norway, February 16, 1952, in a time of 43.2 seconds. It was the same stadium in which Northern track star Cy Perkins had set a record in the 800 meters just five years earlier. When Henry returned to DeKalb, he looked Perkins up and told Cy he had seen his name inscribed on a plaque down inside the stadium. Henry, also a member of the Northern golf team, took time out to serve in the Korean War before returning to DeKalb to complete his degree. He then began a long and successful career in the support of amateur skating in the United States while earning a living as a golf professional at the Park Ridge and Glen Flora Country Clubs.

Another Northern athletic legend, George Bork (at left), led the 1963 football team to a national college division championship. Bork rewrote many of Northern's football records using Hugh Rohrschneider as his favorite target. The last few seasons on the old Glidden Field were among the most memorable ever for Northern football. Rohrschneider, at 6' 6" and 220 pounds, offered a good-sized target for his quarterback. Together they led Northern to the college division championship. In his best season, Rohrschneider caught seventy-six passes. In his junior year, Bork set or broke twenty-six school records, and in the perfect 1963 season, he set NCAA records in eight passing categories. To keep in shape over the winter, Bork played basketball and earned all-league honors while leading the league in scoring at 25.1 points per game. In 1999, Bork became the first NIU athlete inducted into the College Football Hall of Fame.

With cheerleaders cheering, the drum major leading the band, and photographers perched on the roof of Gilbert Hall's entrance, students and fans bid a fond farewell to beloved Glidden Field on the banks of the Kishwaukee. The opening of Huskie Stadium in November of 1965 shifted the focus of men's intercollegiate athletics from the east campus to the west. Construction delays the first half of the 1965 season required the team continue to play at Glidden Field. When the program moved west, groundskeepers transplanted a chunk of its sod to the new field in Huskie Stadium. In the photo below, a student watches one of the last games on Glidden Field from his room in Gilbert Hall.

Glidden Field, 1964

castle on a hill

The closing of Glidden Field and the opening of Huskie Stadium brought a new era to intercollegiate athletics at Northern. Football, always the horse that pulled the wagon, moved from the small college stage to the major university arena. Just as the football program was seeking to reach new heights, another sport at Northern rose to both national and international fame. Coaches Hubert Dunn and Charles Ehrlich turned out more All-Americans and national champions in gymnastics between 1970 and 1990 than any other sport. In fact, in individual competition, NIU has had only five students win NCAA championships, and all were gymnasts from the years 1978 to 1984. Ten NIU gymnasts were named to the All-American team between 1974 and 1987, some of them twice. Many of these athletes and the two coaches who brought them to international attention are now in the Huskie Athletic Hall of Fame.

The two world and Olympic powers in international gymnastics in the 1980s, Japan and the Soviet Union, both sent teams to compete against NIU in Evans Field House. The December 1, 1982, arrival of the Soviet Gymnastics Team was an international event covered by print and electronic media from around the world. Coach Chuck Ehrlich provided the color commentary for SportsVision while assistant coach Lee Battaglia led his team against some of the best gymnasts in the world. A standing-room-only crowd of over 5,000 filled Evans Field House and saw the Russians emerge victorious by a score of 285.3 to Northern's 276.4. NIU's best performance came from the pommel horse where Doug Kieso (left) won the event with a 9.70. Kieso, following in the steps of two-time NCAA national pommel horse champion Mike Burke, became a two-time All-American himself and was crowned NCAA champion in 1983.

One year later, the powerful Japanese national team came to DeKalb, and, again, the field house was packed to overflowing. The Japanese team took home the three top all-around places, but NIU did win the floor exercise event led by Kevin Ekberg with a 9.95, high score for the meet. Olympian Kurt Thomas performed two exhibition routines at this meet that filled the Evans Field House to capacity. Throughout the 1980s, Northern's gymnastic teams continued to turn out All-Americans and national champions.

Pete Botthof, shown here at left, became Northern's first All-American on still rings in 1974. Gymnastics had first been organized as a club sport in 1954 and began to compete as a full-fledged intercollegiate sport in 1957. It was cut completely in March 1990 by an Athletic Board vote of 10–5. The arguments against it were a lower level of high school interest and participation coupled with a decrease across the country as an intercollegiate sport. The issues of costs, budget deficits, and equity under Title IX also played into the decision. In its thirty-three-year run, gymnastics was Northern's most successful sport at the national level.

On the women's side, Canadian Janet Wentworth led NIU's badminton team to national honors. Coach Paul DeLoca recruited Wentworth, from Penticton in British Columbia, to lead the NIU program to a National Association for Intercollegiate Athletics for Women title. Because of a serious ankle injury, Wentworth arrived unseeded at the 1980 tournament but then finished in third place to cement an All-American ranking. That performance also won for Wentworth the national Broderick Award as the top athlete in American badminton. The AIAW annually sponsored championships in thirteen sports.

Here she is seen practicing in Chick Evans Field House. By 1980, women's sports were beginning to change rapidly in the wake of the passage of what became known simply as Title IX in 1972. The federal regulation became effective July 21, 1975, and required that institutions accepting federal funds of any type provide equal opportunities in athletics for men and women. That regulation would, over the course of the next thirty years, change forever the intercollegiate athletic landscape. One of the first changes came with the move of NIU women's athletics from the AIAW to the NCAA.

Perhaps no single issue in sports has been more divisive and important than Title IX. It led to many new opportunities for female athletes at the college and university level that, in turn, opened up new sports and opportunities at the secondary and elementary school levels. In some ways, Northern was ahead of the curve in providing quality programs and facilities for women's athletics, thanks to stalwarts such as Miriam Anderson and Mary Bell, two professors and coaches who built the foundation for women's intercollegiate athletics at NIU. Fully ten years before Title IX became law, NIU built a comprehensive women's sports complex anchored by Anderson Hall. Shown here in an aerial view, a pair of hockey fields and a set of tennis courts border Anderson Hall to the northwest. Farther to the north, a large, open space called the "north forty" lay where cross-country and golf teams could practice. A softball field flanked the parking lots on the east side of the complex. Classrooms, faculty offices, gymnasia, and swimming and diving pools offered state-of-the-art facilities for both physical education classes and intercollegiate athletic competition.

Both the men's and women's swim teams quickly moved from the older, smaller pool in Gabel Hall to their new home. Miriam Mills Anderson, the woman for whom the hall is named, came to Northern in 1928 to establish a major curriculum in physical education for women and served as head of the department until her retirement in 1956. It was Anderson who, during the latter days of her service, dreamed the dreams and did the work necessary to lay the foundation for what women's sports would become in the second half of the twentieth century.

At left the 1937 Daughters of Neptune pose for a team picture beside the pool in the basement of McMurry Hall. Professor Lila Trager, third from right in the back row, was the faculty adviser to the group.

Anderson Hall Swimming and Diving Pools

One of the most common fallacies heard about
Title IX is that it reduced the opportunities for
men while redressing the inequity long experienced
by women. The facts do not bear that out. A
landmark 1996 comprehensive study undertaken
at Northern showed the proportion of women to
men intercollegiate athletes in 1981 was 41
percent to 59 percent. After fifteen years of
Title IX initiatives, the ratio of women to men
was 40 percent to 60 percent. Football, with its
eighty-five scholarships and large teams, skews the
picture and likely always will. There were actually
fewer women's intercollegiate athletic teams at NIU
in 2002 than there were twenty-five years earlier.
Women's gymnastics, while never achieving the
national prominence at NIU the men did, is still
an important minor winter sport on many campuses. Here NIU gymnast Alisha Conahan
competes on the balance beam in a 1998 meet.

While some women's sports such as badminton and field hockey have been
disestablished at NIU, several others have risen to new popularity and none
more than soccer. With the rise of American Youth Soccer Organization
programs across the nation in the 1980s, the interest in and popularity of
women's soccer at the collegiate level was sure to follow. At Northern, the
program could build on an already established, successful men's soccer program
and a new field built just west of Huskie Stadium specifically for soccer.
The women's program soon equaled and then surpassed the men with the
Mid-American Conference title trophy hoisted aloft by Melissa Campbell in
November 1997, just five years after the program began.

(Dan Videtich photograph)

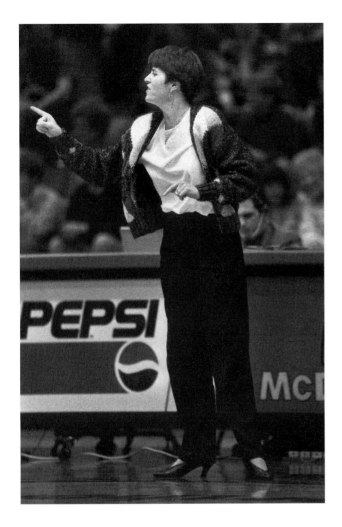

Two new forces entered major intercollegiate athletics in the 1980s and shaped almost all sports in the nineties: corporate sponsorship and extra game spectacle. No longer would the game itself be the sole centerpiece for the fan, nor could a university be competitive without outside funding for athletics. Today, virtually every aspect of athletics from the shoes players wear, to the scoreboard fans check, to the tailgate bandstand has a corporate sponsor advertising for customers. In an age in which pop culture is dominated by Walt Disney and Steven Spielberg, the game is no longer enough to entertain fans. Fireworks, prize giveaways, fan contests, and special entertainment try to keep fans in the seats before, during, and after the game. Any break in game action is an opportunity to shift the focus from the game to temporary amusements.

No sport at NIU more typified the new era than women's basketball under Coach Jane Albright, seen above left framed by the Pepsi and McDonald's advertisements on the scorer's table. She took over the team in 1984, the third coach in four years, and proceeded to build a program of national repute over the next ten years. In her last six years, the NCAA invited Northern to its national tournament five times and the NIT once. National rankings, All-American honors, a large fan base, and corporate support all fell into place as the coach relentlessly pursued the best recruits, took her enthusiasm out to the DeKalb community, and fought quietly but effectively for parity with the men's program. The women's program at Northern showed what twenty years of Title IX, a lot of hard work, good coaching, and maximum enthusiasm could accomplish. When Coach Albright Dieterle left to take the women's head coaching job at the University of Wisconsin, she left behind a record that will be difficult to surpass. In just ten years, her teams put up 188 wins, numerous national rankings, three conference titles, six postseason tournament appearances, and several All-Americans. She also left a legacy of fourteen official corporate sponsors of the program.

One of the best players Coach Albright recruited was Chicago-area native E. C. Hill, shown above right driving to the basket. Hill, along with teammate Cindy Connor, brought Northern back to back 24–6 seasons in the early nineties and signaled a new style for women's basketball at NIU, a tempo and excitement that greatly broadened the fan base for the team. When the women's team moved to the new Convocation Center in the fall of 2002, they invited their old coach to bring her University of Wisconsin team down for the first game and defeated the Badgers.

Over the first half-century, Huskie athletics called the east campus home. For the first twenty-five years, the gymnasium within Altgeld Hall served as home for all indoor athletics. The opening of Still Gymnasium in 1928 provided a much larger and more modern site, and it remained the primary home for intercollegiate athletics until Evans Field House was built. Originally called the Men's Gymnasium, Still was designed to hold a swimming pool but that was cut from the plans because of excessive cost. The post–World War II growth demanded new and more extensive facilities. Chick Evans Field House opened in September of 1957 and, just across the street, Gabel Hall in September 1958. Athletics moved to the center of the campus with the Field House home for most indoor sports and the Gabel Hall pool home for both men's and women's swimming.

Built at a cost of $1.3 million, the Field House offered an indoor track, a basketball court, athletic department offices, and seating for over six thousand. It became home for both men's and women's basketball, wrestling, volleyball, and gymnastics. It also became the venue for annual graduation ceremonies, rock concerts, and trade shows. George "Chick" Evans was the director of Physical Education and Men's Athletics at Northern and had coached, at one time or another, football, basketball, golf, and baseball teams over a period of thirty years.

The move westward into the open farmland on the other side of Annie Glidden Road continued with the building of the dorm complexes in the early 1960s, the creation of an outdoor track, and the opening of Huskie Stadium in the fall of 1965. Nearly a half-century after the Evans Field House had become the home of Huskie sports, the Northern Illinois Convocation Center (above) opened for use in the fall of 2002.

Student fees funded the $36 million Center, which was fifteen years in the making between conception and its opening in October of 2002. The Convocation Center continued the westward push of the Northern campus and became the capstone of a large athletic complex west of Annie Glidden Road. Huskie Stadium, an outdoor track, Mary Bell Field for softball, McKinzie Field for baseball, the NIU soccer fields, the Student Recreation Center, and the Convocation Center gave Northern a complex of athletic facilities as strong as any university its size. The Convocation Center alone occupies a fifty-two-acre site that offers 3,000 parking spaces for those attending events. The arena seats 9,000 for basketball, can provide 60,000 square feet of floor space for trade shows, has a number of hospitality suites, and hopes to host over 150 events each year.

A century after Northern's humble beginnings in 1899, it is still football that lies at the heart of the athletic enterprise of the university's intercollegiate programs. Huskie Stadium, dedicated on November 6, 1965, underwent an extensive remodeling and expansion project in the 1990s and sits at the heart of the west campus athletic complex. For six Saturdays each autumn, it becomes the focus of thousands who come for the pregame tailgating, the socializing, the game, and the fireworks. Workers erect a colorful tent city within the track to the north of the stadium reminiscent of the medieval contests where each tent surrounding the field of battle flew its unique colors and coat of arms. The smoke wafting skyward from roasting meats and the quaffing of great quantities of ale by those who come for the spectacle reinforces the medieval vision.

Fans drive to DeKalb from towns all across northern Illinois and, sometimes, from much farther to see the current crop of warriors do battle with the invaders from some state university to the east. It is Mid-American Conference football.

The spectacle continues well after the game, too. For those early fall night games, the sun has set, the contest has been decided, but the entertainment concludes with a display of brilliant fireworks against the night sky.

The best of the recent warriors was Michael "The Burner" Turner, who became the best of the best when he concluded his career in 2003. Like the knights of old, clad head to foot in modern armor, Turner had extraordinary strength and speed, and, most importantly, undaunted courage and a big heart for battle. Turner led the nation in rushing in 2003 and led his team to a 10–2 season. The Associated Press poll ranked the Huskies as high as twelfth before a loss to Bowling Green. The Huskies of 2003 also brought NIU football to the national stage through games televised on ESPN and Fox SportsNet. Through his accomplishments, Turner took his place alongside such past legends as Reino "The Flying Finn" Nori, Mark Kellar, and LeShon "Cowboy" Johnson. Turner's successor, Garrett Wolfe, led the 2004 Huskies to another outstanding season and their first bowl game in twenty years.

castle on a hill

While it often appears athletics comes first in the modern university, most NIU athletes take good advantage of their opportunity for an education that will serve them for life, long after their athletic prowess has diminished. No NIU athlete of recent times more typifies the ideal combination of brains and brawn than Patrick Stephen. Stephen, a biology major and starting defensive back on the football team, is shown here with an electron microscope in Montgomery Hall. A native of Ontario, Canada, Stephen made 175 tackles in his first twenty-five games as a Huskie and was picked to preseason all-conference honors his senior year in the Mid-American Conference. He also carried a 3.8 grade point average, won the prestigious Arthur Ashe national award, appeared on the cover of Black Issues in Higher Education, *and intends to pursue some field within the medical industry in the future.*

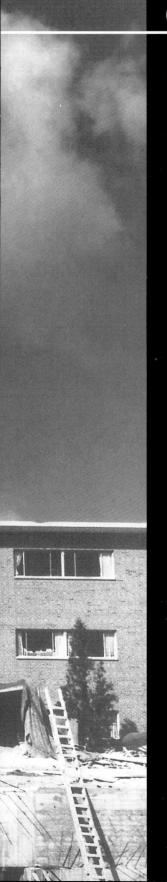

chapter five

CAMPUS DEVELOPMENT

Joseph Glidden donated sixty-three acres of horse pasture along the banks of the Kishwaukee River for a campus in the 1890s when the Illinois Legislature entertained proposals to establish a new Northern Illinois Normal School. The Glidden farm covered nearly eight hundred acres, but the pasture and woods contiguous to the northwest boundary of the city of DeKalb went to the state for a campus. That one decision cast the development of the campus for the next century. With an eastern boundary set by the river and DeKalb residential neighborhoods and a southern boundary established by the railroad and Main Street (Lincoln Highway), there were only two directions in which to grow. For the first fifty years, however, the original acreage sufficed, and it was not until the 1950s that Northern first jumped across Normal Road in what would be a westward expansion that is still ongoing. By the time the campus jumped Normal Road to move west, housing and commercial development had already staked claims to some of the northern boundary along Lucinda Avenue. Campus development came slowly for the first fifty years, but in the 1950s, it then spurted like a teenager as it burst its bounds to the west over and over again.

During its first half-century, Northern built only seven buildings on the campus; in just half that time, from 1950 to 1975, Northern put up thirty-nine major buildings. For the first decade, what is now known as Altgeld Hall was the only building on the campus. It was then known simply as the Northern Normal School, more affectionately as the Castle on a Hill. The school had been created with one purpose in mind: train teachers for area elementary and secondary schools.

It is not surprising, then, that the second building erected on the campus was McMurry Hall (above). One of John Williston Cook's requirements in taking the Northern presidency was that the DeKalb Public Schools would be open to these teachers in training and their trainers. As valuable as on-the-job experience in the DeKalb schools was for students, Cook treasured even more a training school on the campus under the direct supervision of the faculty. Trustees broke ground in 1909 on a plot of land just east of the Castle, and in September 1911, Northern's first training school opened to accept elementary students from DeKalb. The trustees named the building for Cook's star faculty member, Charles McMurry, and his sister-in-law, also on faculty, Lida. Its red brick and its form fit well for the times, and it is still in service almost a century later despite its modest $78,000 price.

For the next fifty years, McMurry served as an elementary laboratory school, and thousands of DeKalb residents built their educational foundation within its walls. On October 23, 1956, Northern broke ground to build a new lab school on the west end of the campus within Gabel Hall. The University Laboratory School opened its doors to students in September of 1958 and it replaced the venerable McMurry School. Unfortunately, the fiscal climate of the early 1970s forced administrators to cut the university's budget, and they made the decision to phase out the laboratory school altogether. In the 1972–1973 school year, the Illinois Board of Higher Education reduced the Lab School's budget by half, effectively ending its life and forcing the students back into the mainstream of the DeKalb Public Schools.

A happier footnote to this history was written in the 1990s when the Shirley Nelson Child Care Center (bottom image) rose just to the west of the old lab school and brought the shouts of young children once again to the playground and lawns surrounding Gabel Hall. The image at top shows the lab school with its students in 1966.

Once the McMurry training school building had been completed, Northern took the important step of building its first dormitory. DeKalb contractors Skogland and Wedberg broke ground on June 3, 1914, and Williston Hall (above) opened to 119 women students in September 1915. Esther Branch, a Kingston native who held an A.B. from Hillsdale College and who had taught at a Normal School in the Philippines, became the first matron. Williston residents lost the freedom of the private boarding clubs, but they now lived only a stone's throw from the library and their classrooms. It was not long before many of the social activities traditional to the clubs became part of the Williston daily life. Residents had the option of waiting tables for the cook, Mrs. Rose, to reduce the cost of living in the dormitory. Trustees used President Cook's middle name, Williston, because Illinois State had already named a building Cook Hall in his honor. Somehow, Williston Hall sounded much better than John Hall.

Employing a strategy that would recur at Northern several times over the coming decades, President J. Stanley Brown decided to use athletics as a means to advance Northern's reputation and to encourage more students to enroll, especially young men. He proposed creating a new building that would house a state-of-the-art gymnasium, a swimming pool, and classrooms specifically targeted to manual and industrial arts. These features, he hoped, would attract young men into the school and thus the teaching profession. The new facility would match McMurry Hall in materials and architecture and be set to the east of the Castle on College Avenue just above the football field and track. In 1925, the Illinois Legislature approved a proposal costing $225,000, cutting Brown's proposal by $50,000. Brown and the Northern trustees cut the swimming pool from the plans and moved ahead. When cutting the pool, however, Brown decided to split the athletic facility from the classrooms, and thus one building became two smaller adjacent structures. The gymnasium would feature a full-sized basketball court and seating for over a thousand spectators. The classrooms now allowed the teaching of wood- and metalworking, mechanical drawing, printing and binding, and the basics of vocational (nonteacher) training. Since the new facility specifically accommodated men's sports, the athletic facilities within the Castle, Brown suggested, should be exclusive to women's athletics. This was the beginning of separate and parallel development of men's and women's athletics.

Built in the same red brick and Bedford stone as McMurry Hall, Still Hall mirrored its collegiate, Gothic architectural style. Like McMurry, Still had two stories above ground and a basement that contained not only the infrastructure necessary to run the building but educational spaces as well. The buildings opened to students on September 10, 1928. The first dance in the new gym took place the evening of Friday, October 19 to kick off Homecoming Weekend. The Northern catalog proudly announced to prospective students "this ensemble of buildings makes a special appeal to young men who are seeking a college that will satisfy their athletic urge and at the same time furnish all modern equipment for industrial training." The only person for whom two buildings are named on the campus, Edgar B. Still was a local pharmacist who also was a member of the Illinois State Normal School Board. Extraordinarily active in the DeKalb community, Still was well known and liked in the area. He also worked tirelessly on the state board to advance projects that would be beneficial to Northern.

The completion of Still Hall marked the beginning of a long hiatus in campus development that carried all the way through the Great Depression of the 1930s and well into World War II. Thus, the campus remained as the Castle on the Hill surrounded by four brick buildings until the addition of a science building in 1943.

President Adams began to press the need for a new building to house the sciences, and, finally, in 1940, the Board committed funds that attracted complementary funding from the Illinois State Legislature in 1941. Northern trustees let the contracts for construction in the spring of 1941. When the U.S. War Production Board inspected the building in progress in 1942, it recommended that all due speed be used to complete it since it was deemed necessary to the interests of the wartime programs.

In architecture, site location, and materials, the new science building marked a new phase in campus development. The collegiate, Gothic style was similar to the buildings of the 1920s, but now the campus clearly was moving westward, and this building was five stories tall. The light-colored flagstone and steel construction, too, marked a departure from Still and Williston Halls and would be used for the next two buildings erected, Adams Hall Dormitory and Swen Franklin Parson Library. Adams Hall and Swen Parson Library, finished within a decade of the opening of the science building, completed the new western boundary of the campus and took Northern up to the residential neighborhood on the west side of Normal Road. Both the science building and Swen Parson Library still faced to the east, with their main entrances completing the third leg of a traditional campus quad. The science building opened to students in the autumn of 1943. Physics and earth sciences found a home on the first floor, home economics on the second, biology on the third, chemistry on the fourth, and meteorology and astronomy on the top floor. Science Hall (above ca. 1945) became William Morris Davis Hall in 1965. Faculty in the earth sciences nominated Davis, the father of the idea of the cycle of erosion and a well-known author and scholar in geography and geology. Today, physics, chemistry, and biology remain centered in this area of the campus in Montgomery and Faraday Halls while Davis Hall houses the geography, geology, and meteorology programs.

ADAMS HALL

The second building planned and built in the 1940s was a badly needed women's dormitory, and campus planners sited it just north of Williston Hall. It faced west and was again similar in architecture to Williston but very different in materials and appearance. This building matched closely Science Hall on the southwest corner of the now expanding campus. Because of the rapidly growing postwar enrollments, President Adams pushed hard for this second dormitory for women students. The Board succeeded in securing an appropriation for what would become Northern's first million-dollar building, and Adams himself broke ground June 24, 1947. He would not live to see the construction completed, as he died suddenly at the age of sixty on December 5, 1948. In honor of his twenty years of service as Northern's president, the Board chose to honor Adams by naming this last building begun under his administration for him. Built to house 120 women students, Adams remained a dormitory for just twenty years before NIU converted it to offices in 1967. Today, it is home for the Graduate School and several other academic programs.

The area from the Kishwaukee River to Normal Road and from Lincoln Highway to Lucinda Avenue is now known as the east campus, but it was the one and only campus for Northern's first half-century, 1899–1949. Thus, the oldest and most treasured campus landmarks and memorials are found on the old east campus. The oldest and most storied of these landmarks is the Freshman Bench in the East Lagoon park. The freshman class of 1903 erected this fieldstone bench as a contribution to the campus on Freshman Day, June 17, 1903. Members of the class built the bench during the night and then dedicated it with a program of oratory under a large oak tree. In the 1950s, the bench became known as the "kissing bench," and several stories have been associated with its history down through the last century.

The second oldest of the campus memorials is the Charles Bench nestled in the dense pines just east of the sidewalk next to Swen Parson Hall. Fred Charles joined the Northern faculty in 1899 at the request of President Cook and promptly made his energetic presence known. He established Northern's biology and botany programs, a student newspaper, and a women's basketball team, which he coached. Within the next several years, Charles also created a large Plant House and a small zoo on the north side of Altgeld Hall. Beloved by the students, Charles left his mark on nearly all who enrolled in that first decade before leaving to take a position at the University of Illinois in 1910. The death of his mother, Dr. Elizabeth W. Charles, sent him into a deep depression in the fall of 1910 from which he never recovered. He died in the early spring of 1911 at the age of thirty-nine, leaving behind a wife and two young daughters. His widow created a scholarship fund in his name at Northern, and after many years, family members asked that the remainder of the fund be used to build a small memorial to him on the campus. In 1943, this bench was placed in the pines and open space just to the north of the new Science Hall. Engraved in the concrete at the foot of the bench is a tribute to his love for his wife and

daughters. In January of 1908, Charles had been asked by President Cook to travel to Chicago to represent Northern at the funeral of a 1902 alumnus who had been killed in a rail accident. Charles began his eulogy with words that well described his own death just three years later: "There come occasions in the lives of most of us when the inscrutable mystery of events overwhelms us with its tragedy and leaves us dumb with awe. Man, erstwhile wont to regard himself as the lord of the universe, awakens to the realization of his utter helplessness and shudders as he wonders at the meaning of it all." The bench keeps alive the legacy of the man who brought a zoo to the schoolchildren of DeKalb a century ago, the beloved professor who founded Northern's science programs.

At the center of the old east campus and on a small hill between the lagoon and the castle sits the Veterans Flagpole. The Northern Illinois Veterans Club collected the private donations required to erect this flagpole in the spring of 1956, and the dedication ceremony shown above left took place June 2, 1956. It is the sole monument to Northern's men and women—faculty, staff, and students—who have served their country in the armed services. Today, the flag still flies day and night as it is lit from below with a spotlight. The State of Illinois flag flies below the Stars and Stripes.

The real showpiece of the markers, memorials, and sculptures to be found on the old east campus is Le Baron, a sixteen-foot-tall stabile set on its own stone pad in the pedestrian quad between Lowden, Davis, and Montgomery Halls and the east lagoon. Contemporary French artist Alexander Calder created the nickel-and-steel structure to mark Rhoten Smith's inauguration as Northern's sixth president. The NIU Foundation purchased the piece for $50,000, and its value thirty years later was estimated at well over $1 million. Many donors contributed to the Foundation's fundraising efforts, the Student Association made the $10,000 down payment, and revenue from vending machines on campus provided the rest of the required funds. Calder designed the piece specifically for this site and then put it on display at the Maison de la Culture in Bourges, France, before dismantling it and shipping it to DeKalb for installation. He personally attended the installation and chose the materials for the base on which it sits. Known as the "man who made sculpture move," Calder's pieces found their place in many public spaces including one at the base of the Sears Tower. He died in 1976 one of the most loved and well known of contemporary artists. Initial reaction to Le Baron was mixed, with many speaking out who were less than appreciative of it. Over time, it has come to be seen as the most important public art on the campus and is treasured by all who come walking from the lagoon to find it waiting in the open tree-lined space.

The 1950s brought rapid increases in enrollment to Northern and a demand for more classroom capacity and administrative offices. The postwar boom also brought a significant change in building architecture to the campus and the end of the large wooded and open spaces to the west of the lagoon. Sharply angular and rectilinear, the new buildings contrasted starkly with the collegiate Gothic of Davis, Swen Parson, Williston, and Adams Halls. The new style first appeared west of Normal Road in the building of Neptune Hall (1955) and Reavis Hall (1957), and first appeared on the old east campus in Faraday Hall, which opened in 1963. The photograph here shows the contrast between the old, Davis Hall, and its new neighbor, Faraday. In the foreground, construction workers lay the foundation for what would become Lowden Hall, the home of presidents and staff for the next forty years.

A close-up of Faraday Hall shot in the dark with the lighting from within shows the best of the new style, which also highlighted new materials in the construction of public buildings. This photograph appeared in the 1964 Norther to showcase the changing times. Modern was in; history was out. Precast concrete had replaced cut stone, and, inside, synthetic materials created by the booming chemical industry had replaced the far more expensive polished marble. Lowden and Montgomery Halls would soon follow the Faraday lead into the new order of style and materials. Virtually all of the buildings created on the old, east campus were of the same genre. When chemistry and physics departments needed space, a $20 million addition to Faraday in the 1990s dropped all ornamentation and produced a factory-like box mimicking the industries driven by the two sciences. Designed by the Chicago firm of Holabird and Root, Faraday II (also known as Faraday West) in photo at bottom offered badly needed classroom and laboratory space for programs that had more than doubled in size since the original Faraday Hall opened in 1964.

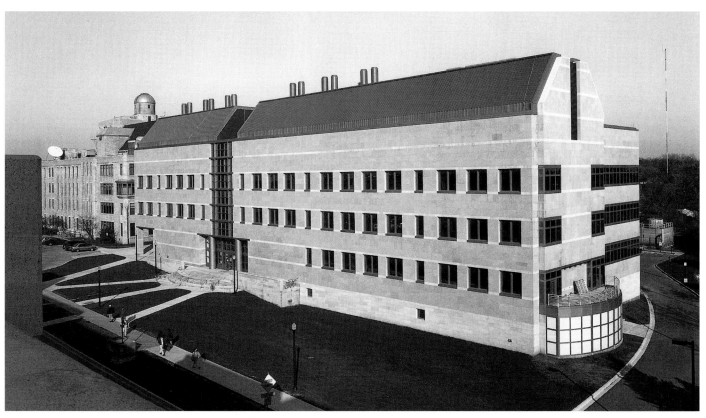

The Health Services Center, built by Johnson, Kile, Seehausen, and Associates of Rockford, brought the construction style of the sixties to an austere and plain climax. A low-rise multistory rectangle with no ornamentation, recessed windows, and built of concrete, the Health Center offered students state-of-the-art medical facilities and staff. According to its director, Dr. Myron W. Larson, "Two big services will add tremendously to the quality of the work and the completeness of diagnostic testing. It should also upgrade the medical practices in our health services and at the same time be a greater convenience to the students." With the completion of the building, the Health Services also added new staff: "five additional physicians, ten nurses, four licensed practical nurses, two x-ray technicians, [a] radiologist, [a] psychiatrist, [a] psychiatric social worker, [a] clinical pathologist, and [an] executive assistant to the director who will handle non-medical and business affairs." What the builders did not know at the time is that thirty years later the entire building would be declared unsafe because of extensive use of asbestos throughout the health facility. After a multimillion-dollar abatement and the necessary long-term relocation, the Health Center is again the clinic of first resort for many NIU students. Today, University Health Services employs ten full-time physicians, a psychiatrist, and two part-time orthopedists for sports medicine. The staff also includes twelve registered nurses, six licensed practical nurses, five medical assistants, three pharmacists, four medical technologists, four professional health educators, two radiographers, one physical therapist, one registered dietician, and thirty-nine support staff. In 1969, the Center had a total of thirty-seven beds and a capacity of fifty-two in its infirmary but by 1992 had eliminated all beds for inpatient service and began to outplace any patients needing hospital care. On average, each year Health Services logs 43,000 patient visits, sees over 12,000 individual students, performs over 34,000 lab tests, and fills about 26,000 prescriptions.

The last open space on the east campus to be used for new construction was the northeast quadrant where the old Glidden Field and track had long stood. With the opening of Huskie Stadium (1965) and a new track to the north of it, the space along the banks of the Kishwaukee was now open for new possibilities. Soon enough, this site became the new home of the fine and performing arts at Northern. These programs were among the largest at Northern and badly crowded the Fine Arts Building (now known as the Stevens Building) from its opening on the central campus in 1959. Construction of a separate home for the visual arts at Northern had been the dream and goal of Professor Jack Arends. The Visual Arts Building, as it was then known, said Arends in 1967, "would provide space for sixty or more faculty plus a rapidly expanding department class enrollment that will total more than 8,000 students this year." When he presided over the setting of the cornerstone for the building in July 1970, Arends proclaimed, "This building will start a golden age for art at Northern Illinois University." The $3 million building gave the university's largest academic department over 100,000 square feet for classrooms, offices, studios, and galleries. For the dedication on April 19, 1971, Michael Straight, deputy chair of the National Endowment for the Arts, spoke of his hope that this facility would "bring art back to the people and beyond the 5 percent of the people in the nation today that enjoy serious art." The thousands of art majors who have spent much of their education in the building and the thousands more who have attended special classes, workshops, and exhibits have brought Northern art to all the people of Illinois and often to audiences well beyond the state. NIU honored Arends's contributions to the art program in 1989, two years after his death, by naming the building for him. Jack Arends came to Northern as the head of the art department in 1962, and, over the next eleven years, he established the BFA and MFA programs, increased the faculty from fourteen to seventy, got the new facility approved and built, and continued to produce his own work as a weaver, designer, and painter.

Shortly after the dedication of the Visual Arts Building, Northern broke ground for a new Music Building on August 31, 1971. Similar in style to the Arts Building, the Music Building, said the architects, "will complement the Art Building and give some unity to this end of the campus. The Music Building will be of concrete and masonry with the colors of these materials either matching or complementing those of its neighbors." The new building stood directly on the banks of the river dividing the campus from the city. Its back door opened to the Lucinda Avenue Bridge that connected town and gown. Since the music programs are one of Northern's strongest bridges to the DeKalb community, the new building offered town residents the opportunity to attend many of the several hundred concerts and recitals offered to the public free of charge each year. This photograph, taken from Lucinda Avenue, shows the open green space between the art and music buildings.

The Boutell Concert Auditorium has been Northern's primary stage for music performance for the past thirty-five years. Musicians and groups from the state, the nation, and the world have performed on this stage from elementary school competitors to world-famous virtuosos. When the hall first opened in 1975, the Plexiglas balls hung from the ceiling to assist in bringing the true sounds from the stage to the audience throughout the hall.

The completion of the fine arts and music buildings nearly filled the original campus acreage. The building of Montgomery Hall on the corner of Lincoln Highway and Normal Road in 1969 completed the complex that served as home to the natural sciences at NIU. With the sciences in one corner, the arts in the opposite corner, the dormitories on the third corner, and the lagoon in the fourth corner, the administrators took the center with space in Lowden and Altgeld Halls. While the old, east campus was filling, Northern had already begun to acquire property to the west and north and began expansion into what would eventually become the central campus and the west campus areas. There was, however, one more little piece of real estate that Northern's trustees had secured to add to the original sixty-three acres Joseph Glidden had donated: Jimmie's Tea Room just across the College Avenue Bridge on the banks of the river and the lagoon. Jimmie's is a rich part of Northern lore, and the building still stands today as a tribute to the post–World War II period of history.

"On Saturday, September 9, [1940,] the new college eating place on College Avenue just east of the bridge served its first customers. Its proprietor, Jimmie Lundberg, hopes to fill a need which was felt on this campus by providing a grand and pleasant eating establishment." Thus was born Northern's first student center. Named the College Tea Room, the place quickly enough became just plain old "Jimmie's," and it served as Northern's student union for twenty years until the opening of the University Student Center on campus in 1962. The Illinois Teachers College Board approved purchase of Jimmie's in 1948 and issued $60,000 in bonds to effect the transfer from private to public ownership. Jimmie's was the campus social center for generations of Northern students, and the building later served as home for WNIU-FM, the Northern Star, and as offices for the School of Art. Since its acquisition, it has been known as Jimmie's Tea Room, WNIU-FM, Roy G. Campbell Hall, and now as Kishwaukee Hall. Jimmie's primary competition at the time of its acquisition was the Prince Castle hamburger stand on nearby North First Street. As seen here, Prince Castle offered a seven-cent hamburger in the summer of 1946.

Right behind Jimmie's, reaching high into the DeKalb skyline, sits the main transmission tower for WNIU-FM. Established in 1954 as educational noncommercial station WNIC-FM, the station changed its call letters to WNIU-FM in 1968 and expanded to a full spectrum of programming that featured educational as well as entertainment content. The station also provided an opportunity for students to get practical experience in broadcast media. In 1974, the station increased its power from 2,500 to 50,000 watts and, two years later, built the 300-foot transmission tower that still stands in Jimmie's backyard. While building the tower, two steeplejacks, Bob Balwanz and Richard Cross, narrowly escaped serious injury when an 800-pound section of the tower broke loose in what was termed a "freak accident." "If it would have hit a guy wire, the tower might be down now," a shaken Bob Balwanz said just moments after the section broke loose and crashed through a chain link fence surrounding the base of the new tower. Cross and Balwanz were both up on the tower, said Cross, when he "unfastened the top saddle to bolt the gin pole to the tower [and] a greasy cable slipped from his hand and he was unable to prevent the gin pole from breaking loose."

This aerial photograph below taken in 1959 shows Glidden Field still in place (lower right) and also shows the first buildings west of Normal Road in what is now known as the central campus. The small cross in the upper right center is the foundation for Married Student Housing, the first facility built west of Annie Glidden Road. Only the smokestack behind Altgeld Hall could be seen more than a block from the campus, but that would change in the coming decade as Northern began to build up as well as out. By 1969, people traveling to NIU from out on the prairie could see the silhouette of the campus skyline from many miles away.

Watson East Construction, 1966

When erected in 1967, the radio tower became the tallest structure on the campus, but the building of the central and west campuses in the 1960s brought the first high-rise buildings to DeKalb. The first facilities built west of Normal Road, Reavis Hall (1957), Evans Field House (1957), and Neptune Dormitory (1959), featured the usual low-to-the-ground architecture. By the mid-sixties, however, the skyline on the campus had begun to form with the building of a ten-story faculty office complex known as Watson East (now Zulauf Hall) and the dormitories surrounded by cornfields west of Annie Glidden Road. Watson East became the home for the largest of NIU colleges, the College of Liberal Arts and Sciences, with each of the ten floors housing a different department's office and faculty. After thirty-five years, it remains home to the college.

At the same time the Watson East tower began to rise into the sky, the University Center added a tower of guest rooms on the west end of the building. Construction on the first phase of the University Center began with groundbreaking on December 8, 1960. After two years of construction, the students had, for the first time, a home away from home in the middle of the campus. Here they could find a place to relax in lounges, have fun in the bowling alleys, find a quiet place to study, or meet friends in the cafeteria for a coke and a burger. The showpiece of the new center was the Carl Sandburg Auditorium, which would serve as the primary venue on campus for large public lectures and professional fine arts performances for the next four decades. Chicago legend Studs Terkel and Sandburg's granddaughter Paula Steichen spoke at the dedication. Forty years later, Terkel returned to NIU for an evening of entertainment, and, once again, he took the stage on which he had performed in 1963. Every Northern student has some fond memories of time spent in the University Center whether in the auditorium, the ballroom, the bowling alleys, or, now, watching soap operas in the lounges. Over the years, a number of enterprises have come and gone within the Center's walls. The cafeterias and restaurants have changed many times; today, McDonald's sits at the center of student interest in the lower level, and there are both automatic teller machines dispensing instant cash throughout the building and a full service bank on site.

(Luci Jordao photograph)

University Center Construction, 1967

Just six years after opening the main portion of the building, work began on the tower of guest rooms, which today is the landmark seen all the way out to the interstate highway. The tower was completed in May 1968. Expanding the building by 345,000 square feet, the sixteen-story tower cost nearly $10 million to build, but, noted the university publicists of the time: "No tax money is involved in either the construction of the facilities or the operation." Student fees were to pay off the bonds that underwrote the construction of this hotel operation. Just twenty years later, pieces falling from the exterior walls of the building presented such a safety hazard, the entire building had to be reclad with 2,000 limestone panels, and, at that time, designers added the pyramid-shaped cupola to house heating and air conditioning equipment. Northern trustees named the complex for retired President Leslie Holmes in April of 1974 as part of the university's celebration of its seventy-fifth anniversary.

Because of its imposing height, the Holmes Student Center tower is the defining landmark for the campus. At 235 feet and with ridge lighting on the top, the Center can be seen for many miles across the prairie in the night sky. Another landmark of the central campus, much less imposing but equally important, is the postal kiosk (left) through which generations of NIU students have sent letters home. Built as part of the boom of the mid-sixties, the kiosk today remains an important stop for students as they make their way across the campus. Electronic automation has replaced the old mechanical system, but the purpose is the same, and daily use remains high.

The construction of the Martin Luther King Jr. Mall between the Founders Library and the Holmes Student Center in the 1980s brought the opportunity to showcase public sculpture at the heart of the campus. Two sculptures, one modern and one traditional, speak to the thousands of students and staff who cross through this heart of the campus each day. Sculptor Peter Fagan donated the bronze bust of King in the foreground in 1993 when the mall was completed. Illinois State University sculptor Dan Nardi created the large black and white concrete sculpture in the background and titled it Balance of Equality. The base is annually planted in flowers, and bronze plates with quotations from King surround the monument. A national competition produced Nardi's winning entry.

Minneapolis sculptor Steven Beyer created one large public sculpture that began its life at Northern on the King Commons. Table of Six Questions, forty-eight feet in length, attracted instant attention. Built of heavy Corten steel, this sculpture, like most introduced to the campus, also generated more than a little discussion. The Wall Street Journal ran a page-one story October 19, 1981, that began: "The students at Northern Illinois University in rustic DeKalb, Illinois, may not be connoisseurs of modern art, but they know what they don't like." The story also reported: "[A]s the crane lowered the sculpture into place, students gathered to jeer, and a young man later tried to deface the work. He kicked it from beneath, jumped up and down on it, and only stopped after knocking off a piece of metal. The piece was welded back into place." The six questions cut into the top of the table? "Do you need a bath?"; "Are you going home?"; "Do you cry?"; "Have you been introduced?"; "What is your next move?"; and "Do you know the facts?" In actuality, they appear without punctuation and read in ascending order of complexity. The questions, according to Beyer, reflect psychologist Abraham Maslow's hierarchy of human needs. Art professor Ben Mahmoud suggests that "as we sit at the table, returned to our childhood, we read the texts that progressively move us through the simpler questions to interrogatives that are more adult. . . . As is the case with most postmodern work, the interpretation is open." Over time, the piece was moved to an open space near the west lagoon, the controversy over it has subsided, and it has become an important part of the constellation of public sculptures on the Northern campus. As for the initial controversy, Beyer said, "everything can't be pretty to the eye. Art is no exception. How a piece of art looks is not my main concern when I create art. I'm interested in creating an impression to something I've seen or experienced."

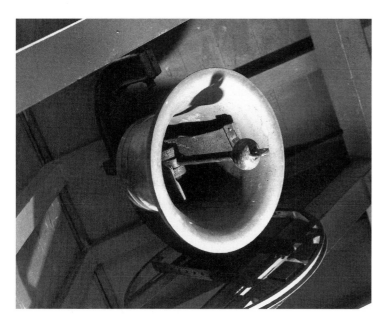

In 1957, Alpha Phi Omega service fraternity initiated a drive to obtain a victory bell for NIU to give Northern "a tradition rich in purpose and to promote good sportsmanship and fair play." With proceeds from its Ugliest Man on Campus contest in 1958, the APO Victory Bell Committee purchased a bell (top left) from a local rural school. Two Victory Bell Committee members are seen here (top right) looking over the bell after it arrived at the physical plant for some rehabilitation before being set out for public view. Set in a foundation of brick, stone, and timbers erected on Malus Island across from Gabel Hall, the bell has been rung after athletic victories for the past forty years. Dedicated October 8, 1960, the Victory Bell first rang to celebrate a football win over Eastern Illinois.

Most of the construction of the 1960s took place on what would become known as the central campus, that area bounded by Normal Road on the east, Annie Glidden Road on the west, Lucinda Avenue on the north, and Lincoln Highway on the south. While the boom on the central campus continued to accelerate, Northern lost no time in jumping Annie Glidden Road to begin work on what would become the west campus. The large footprint of Huskie Stadium established the direction for future growth, and the first two high-rise dormitories, Grant Towers, climbed into the prairie sky the same time as the stadium. There was enough concurrent construction across all three areas of campus that the Norther yearbook ran this photo (at left) in 1965.

Grant Towers, 1965

With Watson East and the new tower added to the University Center, Northern made a statement that it would pursue vertical as well as horizontal expansion to meet the needs of a university student population that had grown far faster than the physical facilities. The wide-open spaces of the cornfields west of Annie Glidden could have accommodated the sprawl of many low-rise dormitories on the model of Gilbert and Neptune, but each new building took students farther away from their classrooms, laboratories, and the library. Maintaining proximity to the central area of the campus was a priority for planners. Two matching sets of high-rise dorms, Grant and Stevenson, complemented the more traditional low-rise Douglas and Lincoln Halls. Each consisted of four matching thirteen-story towers. This area became the focus of dormitory living at NIU once all the buildings had been opened.

Physical Plant Loading Dock
Frozen Foods Locker

In the 1960s, the west campus also became the home for the infrastructure needed to service and maintain the rapidly growing university and campus. The physical plant provided space for materials delivery and management, campus postal operations, the many craftsmen and shops needed to maintain the buildings, and for the automobiles and buses needed to move faculty, staff, and students. When enrollment totaled only 2,285 in 1953, two mechanics and a small Quonset hut behind Williston Hall were enough to keep the few vehicles running as seen in these photographs (top and above right).

The size and scope of university operations increased in proportion to the 800 percent rise in enrollment over the next ten years, and the new Physical Plant met the new needs. Opened as Northern's first major building west of Annie Glidden, the Physical Plant loading docks could handle multiple loads from semitrailer trucks and provided a large facility for fleet storage and maintenance.

As the west campus was expanding and the central campus began to fill, Northern continued to buy properties contiguous to the campus as often as possible. The first purchases were the private residences along Normal Road that divided the older, east campus from the newer, central area. There was little resistance to Northern's efforts, but as the private residences began to vanish, a new phenomenon rose in the early 1960s that remains today. Normal Road from Lincoln Highway on the south to Greek Row on the north became the home for most campus religious ministries. Many of these began when local churches purchased private homes near the campus in which to offer students a place to congregate, study, socialize, and worship. One of the first of these was the Methodist-related Wesley Fellowship. Pictured here is the Wesley Foundation House at 205 Normal Road in the early spring of 1958. The Wesley Fellowship eventually sold this house to NIU and built a church just west of this property on the corner of Carroll Avenue and West Locust where it remains. That church is the only piece of property on the central campus not owned by NIU today. The home pictured here is now part of the parking lot just south of Founders Memorial Library.

Lutheran Chapel, 1958

First Lutheran Church of DeKalb also purchased a two-story brick home in which to begin ministry to NIU students on campus in 1957, this one just one long block north on Normal Road just past Lucinda. The church had hired a graduate assistant to work with students, and this home, Luther House, provided not only a place to congregate and study but also dormitory rooms for sleeping and a kitchen that boarders shared with the resident assistant. With a major remodeling, the garage behind the house became the first Lutheran Chapel for Northern students, and the congregation called a pastor who was to spend one third of his time working to develop the campus ministry.

In 1959, Lutheran Campus Ministry (LCM), now getting support from the national campus ministry of the Lutheran Church in America, purchased the land just to the south of Luther House on the northwest corner of Lucinda and Normal for $45,000. LCM built the current facility on that site and opened its doors in 1975. For a few years, it shared the building with another Normal Road campus ministry, Judson Fellowship and Baptist Campus Ministry. Judson Fellowship had also begun in a home on Normal Road, that of Pastors John and Ruth Peterson. Less than ten years after moving in to share the LCM building, however, Baptist Campus Ministry had its own new church and fellowship building just up the road at 449 Normal Road. Set between these two new buildings on Normal Road on the east side of the street was the largest of all campus ministries, the Newman Center.

The Newman Center (right) is not only the largest of the Normal Road ministries, it is a truly town and gown parish. Professor Marguerite O'Conner first approached Father Charles Quinn at DeKalb's St. Mary's Church in 1941 with a request to begin a Newman Club on the campus. The first meeting attracted twelve students, who met at the St. Mary's rectory. In the 1950s, Father Charles McCarren raised and borrowed enough money to purchase an old house at 618 College Avenue that was home for the growing student group until 1960. In 1957, Father McGinn bought several acres of land with a farmhouse on it and, with the support of Bishop Loras T. Lane and the Knights of Columbus, the Newman group built the current facility. The ministry earned full parish status in 1966 under the title Christ the Teacher University Parish. At the northern end of Normal

Road, those students seeking an Episcopalian expression of faith will find the Canterbury Fellowship within St. Paul's, and those of Islamic faith can find the NIU Islamic Center at 721 Normal Road. The only two campus ministries not located on Normal Road are found on Russell Road, one block west: the Northern Illinois Jewish Community Center and Immanual Lutheran Church–Missouri Synod also reach out to Northern's students, faculty, and staff.

While the primary direction of campus development had always been to the west, for more than three decades following World War II, the university did own a large parcel of land to the north of the original campus. Right after the war, Northern administrators secured a large group of army barracks from Camp McCoy in northern Wisconsin and moved them to the north side of Lucinda, just west of the river, to serve as temporary housing for the flood of returning veteran students. The first major facility built to the north was Anderson Hall, the anchor for a women's athletic complex. For twenty years, the large open space to the north and east of Anderson was known simply as the "north forty." When the university acquired the land, the hope was that it would become a golf course, and, in fact, landscape architects drew plans for that purpose. The golf course

never materialized, and the land sat open as a university park and recreation area until Northern established a College of Engineering and Engineering Technology in 1984. After living for a few years in a temporary home in a remodeled Sycamore industrial plant, NIU broke ground on the north forty for a new Engineering Building, July 21, 1993 (above).

The university had expanded its north forty holding in 1987 with the purchase of the Palmer Music Building on the southeastern border of the property. That purchase not only gave Northern a new home for its radio stations—it became the NIU Broadcast Center—but it afforded access from First Street in DeKalb, an important strategic advantage. Once the plans for a golf course moved from hope to the archives, the north forty offered a new place for possible building and expansion of student and academic programs. The old, east campus bounded by the river, Lincoln Highway, and Normal Road began to push northward. A new home for many student activities and organizations went up on the northeast corner of Lucinda and Normal. The Campus Life Building opened in March of 1995 and afforded a home for such programs as Student Orientation, Honors, Counseling and Student Development, the Campus Activities Board, and the Northern Star. Its central location and proximity to the Holmes Student Center served students well. The view in the photograph is from the main lobby of the Campus Life Building looking to the southwest and the Holmes Student Center across the street.

In 2000, Northern alumnus Dennis Barsema and his wife, Stacey, decided to make the single largest donation for development in NIU history. They gave the university stock in a company Dennis had founded valued at $24 million. The sale of the stock provided the funds necessary for a new home for the College of Business. The photo here shows the east side of the newly opened hall in 2002. Barsema Hall was the third major building erected on the old north forty, and, set side by side with the newly opened Engineering Building, it spoke of the future. Engineering and business, hand in hand, had become the front-running academic programs at Northern over the last several decades of the twentieth century. Now each had a new home, and they were campus neighbors. Courses in both colleges were much in demand not only by students residing on the DeKalb campus but by many more who spent evenings upgrading their knowledge at Northern's outreach centers in Rockford, Hoffman Estates, and Naperville.

Just as Governor Altgeld brought education out to the various parts of the state in the 1890s, so Northern in the 1990s built two satellite facilities to bring classes closer to two of the larger population centers in its service region. Many of Northern's students want to work and take classes at the same time, and these centers fill a large demand, especially for upper-level undergraduate and graduate-level classes. Working in partnership with the Sears Company and local political entities, Northern secured a gift of land that was part of the large new Sears headquarters just off the Northwest Tollway. After breaking ground in October of 1991, the $6 million project moved quickly and celebrated with a grand opening just one year later in October of 1992. The Hoffman Estates facility offered conference and training facilities to area businesses and organizations as well as a venue at which the many classes NIU had been offering in the western suburbs could be consolidated. The success of the Hoffman Estates Campus was such that NIU was already looking to expand on a twenty-acre site nearby that a developer pledged as a donation in 1998.

FIRST SEMESTER, 1939-40
Northern Illinois State Teachers College, De Kalb, Illinois
EXTENSION CLASSES
(Classes were held for the first time last week)

City	Course	Place and Time of Meetings	Instructor
Aurora	Speech 106	East Aurora H.S., Mondays, 4:15 P.M.	Dr. Yonkam
Downers Grove	Music 310	Washington School, Mondays, 4:30 P.M.	Miss Slansland
Harvard	Mathematics 300	High School, Mondays, 5:00 P.M.	Mr. Stowe
Mt. Carroll	Education 216	High School, Mondays, 8:00 P.M.	Mr. Peterson
Ottawa	Biol. Sci. 104	Shabbona School, Mondays, 4:00 P.M.	Dr. Montgomery
	Soc. Sci. 260	Shabbona School, Mondays, 7:00 P.M.	Dr. Jameson
DeKalb	Education 215	Room 117, N.I.S.T.C., Tuesdays, 7:00 P.M.	Mr. Peterson
Freeport	Ind. Arts 240	Junior High School, Tuesdays, 7:00 P.M.	Mr. Oakland
Joliet	Education 405	Central School, Tuesdays, 4:30 P.M.	Dr. Howell
Lena	Fine Arts 301-302	High School, Tuesdays, 7:40 P.M.	Miss Wiggert
McHenry	Music 310	High School, Tuesdays, 4:30 P.M.	Miss Slansland
	Speech 106	High School, Tuesdays, 7:05 P.M.	Mr. Dehl
Aurora	Education 341-342	West Aurora H.S., Thursdays, 7:20 P.M.	Dr. Messenger
Geneva	Phys. Educ. 300-301	Court House, Thursdays, 7:00 P.M.	Miss M. Andersen
Rockford	Phys. Educ. 300-301	Senior High School, Thursdays, 4:30 P.M.	Miss Cain
Waukegan	Soc. Sci. 260	Library, Thursdays, 4:30 P.M.	Dr. Whittaker
	English 280	Library, Thursdays, 7:00 P.M.	Mr. Connor
Yorkville	Soc. Sci. 260	High School, Thursdays, 7:00 P.M.	Mr. Estnof

Just as the Hoffman Estates Center served to focus and consolidate Northern's activities in the northeast part of NIU's service region, the Rockford Education Center (top) did so for the northwestern area. Although Rockford Mayor Charles Box preferred a downtown site, Northern balanced the interests of all who would use the facility and chose the site on the far southeast side near the interstate highway. Built at a cost of $6 million, the 40,000-square-foot facility is home not only to NIU classes but also to many social and educational activities of Rockford area businesses and organizations. The Center opened in the autumn of 1995. The two centers are just twenty miles apart and linked directly to I-90, a main artery between Chicago and Rockford.

The building of these two extension centers in the 1990s demonstrated the university's commitment to bringing classes out into the region it serves. Distance education classes taught on the Internet and an agreement to teach upper-level classes at Rock Valley College in 2002 have significantly increased the commitment to outreach. Extension programs, however, have a long history at Northern dating back to 1939 when the first classes offered off-campus were taught at area high schools.

Northern, in the 1960s, expanded its extension program to some of the state correctional facilities in the northern region of the state. A program had begun using Chicago public television station WTTW in 1958 to offer the first two years of college to inmates. Northern then entered the program to offer the third year of undergraduate work on site by sending professors into prisons at Stateville, Sheridan, Dwight, and Pontiac. With some special support from the Illinois Board of Higher Education, the NIU College of Continuing Education expanded the classes offered. In 1976, the university instituted the Bachelor of General Studies (BGS) degree so that residents of correctional centers could obtain a degree without having to specialize in one area. It proved nearly impossible, for example, to offer lab-based science classes on site. Many faculty members found teaching in the prisons to be rewarding, and some of their best students were inmates. These were often very active, even aggressive, learners who wanted to soak up new information and were not afraid to challenge and be challenged. The photograph above shows a German class being taught at the Joliet State Penitentiary in 1967. The NIU Prison Program ended in the winter of 1988 when the state required drug testing for all entering the prison and Provost Kendall Baker said, "Testing teachers is a presumption of guilt. . . . We can choose not to participate." Provost Baker also disestablished the entire College of Continuing Education during his four-year tenure at Northern.

The antithesis of the adult prison programs were the outdoor education programs offered to elementary school children at the Lorado Taft Campus in Oregon, Illinois. Soon after he arrived at Northern, President Leslie Holmes convinced area legislators to work for the acquisition of a branch campus in Oregon, Illinois. State Senators Dennis Collins (DeKalb) and Charles W. Baker (Davis Junction) introduced a bill in 1951 to give Northern a sixty-six-acre site for outdoor teacher education adjacent to the Lowden State Park along the Rock River. This tract, the northwest corner of Lowden State Park, included the original fifteen-acre site of the Eagles Nest Colony. Chicago sculptor Lorado Taft had established the colony in 1898. The buildings of Eagles Nest had been abandoned in 1942, six years after Taft's death, and several of the sculptures still remained on the grounds. One of the most well-known landmarks in western Illinois is Taft's great concrete statute of Chief Blackhawk standing high above the Rock River on land adjacent to the Lorado Taft Campus. Completed in 1910, this massive work may be Taft's best-known piece. Taft, a nationally prominent sculptor, first came to spend summers here in the 1890s, and for nearly a half-century, Chicago artists followed the trail west to Eagles Nest high above the river. In this photograph above, students inspect one of the life-sized sculptures on the grounds titled Druid Funeral Procession. It depicts six Druid priests bearing a sarcophagus. Taft's magnum opus, however, would dwarf the lifelike sculptures found in the woods on the grounds. Having taken the idea for a tall, concrete statue from two concrete chimneys he had seen erected at the Art Institute of Chicago heating plant, Taft enlisted engineer Leland Summers and a student, John Prasuhn, to help him. Twenty-eight laborers participated in the construction during December of 1910, mixing and pouring concrete for ten consecutive days. By spring, the statue had set, and on July 1, 1911, a large crowd traveled to Oregon for the unveiling and dedication. It is the largest public monument honoring Native Americans in the state of Illinois. Although Taft did not fashion this sculpture specifically to resemble or honor Chief Blackhawk, it came over time to bear his name.

Fifty years after acquiring the Lorado Taft Campus, the university disestablished its graduate degree program in outdoor teacher education. Still today, however, the programs to teach area elementary students about the outdoors through field trips to the campus continue.

chapter six

LIVING IN DEKALB

During the 1960s, the central and west campuses grew rapidly and filled the area from Lincoln Highway on the south to Lucinda Avenue on the north and from Normal Road on the east to and across Annie Glidden Road on the west. The Kishwaukee River, Lincoln Highway, and residential housing patterns determined that growth would be ever westward. This growth pattern also brought the usual development of private businesses catering to students at the boundaries. Both Lincoln Highway and Lucinda Avenue became commercial strips in the sixties and remain so today. Fast-food restaurants, bookstores, convenience marts, hair salons, and laundromats have sprung up, disappeared, and reappeared under new ownership for the past forty years. One of the first student favorites to appear on Lincoln Highway was McDonald's. True to its marketing genius, McDonald's claimed the spot at the center of campus on the north side of Lincoln Highway in 1960 and has never left. After forty years, the owners razed the original building and replaced it with a new one. The golden arches have stood on this site now for nearly a half-century. This first DeKalb McDonald's, 805 West Lincoln Highway, opened before the advent of drive-through service but continued to update and expand and is still thriving today. In the 1980s, a second

Lincoln Highway McDonald's, 1976

McDonald's followed on Lincoln Highway just east of downtown, then one on Sycamore Road, another out on the I-88 tollway, and finally, inevitably, McDonald's took over food service in the NIU Holmes Student Center Powwow Room in 1995. For providing space in the Student Center, NIU received 8 percent of the revenues, which amounted to about $40,000 a year when the restaurant first opened. The lease was for ten years, according to then Vice President Jim Harder: "We solicited proposals from various brand fast-food franchises. This was the best proposal we got. We have to believe McDonald's knows their business." Why contract out? "We were trying to respond to customer desire," Harder added. "Our students today have grown up with branded-type products." But even that was not the end, as a sixth McDonald's opened in the Village Commons Shopping Center on Lucinda Avenue. Students on campus had easy walking access to three of the golden arches within blocks of one another.

The West Lincoln Highway strip featured many, many popular restaurants over the years, and three of the more popular and long-lived were Tom and Jerry's, Sergeant Pepper's, and the Junction Eating Room, which featured, respectively, Greek, Italian, and American menus.

Two local entrepreneurs, Tom Rosenow and Jerry Blessing, opened their restaurant in 1974 but eventually sold it to John Pappas. In the winter of 1988, Pappas purchased the Dairy Queen building just a block west at 215 West Lincoln Highway and built a new, larger facility of 1,600 square feet that would seat fifty. Pappas also purchased the lot next to the Dairy Queen for parking and hoped to acquire the John Street cul de sac from the city of DeKalb. Bob Daughter, owner of the Dairy Queen, had not had a buyer until Pappas called him "one day out of the blue." Just eight months earlier, Pappas had opened a second Tom and Jerry's at 1670 DeKalb Avenue, halfway to Sycamore. He would open another Tom and Jerry's in Rochelle and several in the Rockford area. Known especially for their gyros, Tom and Jerry's soon added a small fleet of trucks and offered delivery service throughout the city. Today, each of the restaurants is independently owned.

As much a fixture in student eating habits as any of the Lincoln Highway places was the Junction Eating Place in the Junction Shopping Center just across Lincoln Highway from the first McDonald's. Frank Day opened the restaurant in 1969, and it has remained a favorite of faculty and students for thirty-five years. The restaurant was also the gateway to a number of businesses within the rest of the shopping center over the years. The west section of the Center was built in 1979. Among the longer-lasting and better-known Junction Center businesses were Finn's Clothing Limited, the Junction Book Room, Baskin Robbins Ice Cream, a hair salon that changed owners several times, the Junction Center Laundromat, and Video Plus, a video rental store. Set alongside the tracks of the Chicago North Western, the Junction Center used a railroad motif in its external facades and advertising. The front door to the restaurant, pictured here in 1976, matched the rear appearance of a caboose.

Perhaps no other restaurant on the Lincoln Highway strip generated more memories for NIU students, staff, and alumni over the past half-century than Sergeant Pepper's on the corner of Lincoln Highway and Annie Glidden Road. Home of the famous beer nuggets, Sergeant Pepper's carries the name of one of the Beatles's most famous albums from the 1960s. For its grand opening September 10, 1976, Sergeant Pepper's featured a long list of sandwiches at one dollar each, a quarter-pound hamburger for eighty cents, and a free drink with every order. The original owners sold the restaurant in 1995 to Chris and Mike Carpenter, who owned two nearby bars. They reopened it in July of 1996 and then, in turn, sold it to Artie Alberts, who changed the name to RT's in 2001.

Local real estate developer and businessman Joseph Katz owned much of the land north of the NIU campus between Annie Glidden and Russell Roads with the exception of the Immanuel Lutheran Church property. The land along Lucinda Avenue would become the most valuable real estate in DeKalb once it was rezoned for commercial use in 1967. In January of 1968, Katz succeeded in getting the city council to grant him a special use permit to construct what would become the Village Commons. "We plan to have the shopping center completed in time for the '69 school year," Katz said, and the center would include "a bookstore, a women's fashion store, a drug store, a men's haberdashery, a shoe store, a music shop, a dress wear rental, a sporting goods store, a dry cleaner, and a pizza parlor." Both NIU and local businessman Sam Brody tried to stop the development of the Village Commons but failed in their attempts to keep the space open. Brody filed suit claiming that zoning and permit regulations had been violated, but the local courts ruled in Katz's favor. As the sign in this photograph shows, Katz worked with one of the giants of Chicago area commercial development, Arthur Rubloff and Company. Local businessman Richard Boardman first owned the bookstore and then, in 1987, became the owner of the entire VCB property.

Over the past thirty-five years, many businesses have come and gone from the Village Commons, but the bookstore, the fast-food outlets, and the convenience stores have been the staples that attract student business year in and year out. The Village Commons Bookstore has provided the only major competition for the University Bookstore in supplying texts for courses and other common student office supplies.

Sandwich shops and pizza parlors have always done well in attracting student customers though the names have changed often through the years. Just as fast-food vendors dominate the southern edge of the campus along Lincoln Highway, the same is true for the northern edge along Lucinda in the Village Commons. Pictured here is the Village Commons Subway franchise photographed in 1997. Another Subway outlet can be found on Lincoln Highway across from the lagoon.

One of the objections filed against the Katz special use permit to build the Commons related to a release from the obligation to provide adequate parking for customers. Arthur Rubloff, the leasing firm, said "the local ban on student use of motorized vehicles" was the reason they felt no need to provide parking. "We chose the area across from the Field House because it was in the traffic pattern of the students. In bad weather, it will be a convenience for those students without cars who live on the west side of campus," Katz argued. "Also, if a parking lot is built, many students would park all day, go to classes, and never shop in the center." Eventually, the Village Commons did build a small lot just to the east of the shopping center.

University Plaza Construction, 1966

Immanuel Lutheran Church, through the bequest of a parishioner, owns a large parcel of land directly north of the Village Commons, and it stretches all the way from Annie Glidden Road to Russell Road. Directly north of that, Katz again owned the land together with Ralph Mickelson and Morton Crane. They had purchased it from Annie Glidden in September of 1965 to develop it with students in mind. From the beginning, Northern students had found housing in private accommodations off the campus. The University Plaza was the first large private sector dormitory built for student housing.

While the University Plaza succeeded in providing an alternative to university-owned dormitory housing, other attempts to create private dorms farther from the campus failed. Once again, as in all real estate, location was the key, and the University Plaza was just one long block from the center of the campus and fell between the campus and the newly developing Greek Row (above) to the north. Joseph Katz also owned the land just to the north of the University Plaza dormitories, and on it he developed the apartment complexes known collectively as University Village in the 1970s. Beyond the University Village lay the open land that in the 1960s became Greek Row for Northern Illinois University. Even before Katz broke ground for the University Plaza in 1965, several sororities and fraternities with national affiliation had begun to build in the wide-open farmlands several blocks to the north.

Over the next thirty years, these open fields became the home to more Greek houses and many apartment complexes. The ever-increasing population density enticed the commercial development that followed. Here, too, student-oriented businesses predominated: movie theaters, fast-food franchises, convenience marts, laundromats, and a combination liquor store/tavern.

Once the Greek Row area was filled, the first Greek house to jump west of Annie Glidden was Delta Phi Epsilon in 1992. The local Delta Phi chapter had rented a house at 918 Kimberly Drive for ten years from the inactive Alpha Phi Omega sorority. When Alpha Phi Omega again built an active NIU chapter, the Delta Phi sorority built the first house west of Annie Glidden. Just as the sixties had brought rapid development east of Annie Glidden, the nineties would bring new student housing complexes and student-related businesses to the west side of the street. By the year 2000, student housing and commercial development had surrounded the NIU campus on three sides and only the west was still open for further campus expansion. As the 1990s came to a close, New Hope Baptist Church and the Eden's Garden Housing development made the jump to the north side of Twombly Road along Annie Glidden. Eden's Garden brought hundreds of moderate-cost housing units to the local residential market.

In March of 1971, Northern students approved a referendum that called for a $7 increase in the student activity fee to provide for a bus system both on and off the campus. Two months later, the Board of Regents approved the idea and put the newly created bus system out for bids. The American Transit Company in St. Louis offered the low bid, and the following year, the system began with ten buses running five routes through the NIU campus and the city. There were some complaints from city officials about the damage the heavy buses would do to the city streets, but businesses and apartment owners throughout the city favored high student mobility. The buses initially ran only Monday through Friday and from 7:00 a.m. to 11:00 p.m. In two years, the fee had risen to $10 per semester, and the contract was valued at over $300,000. In 1973, the drivers attempted to organize with the local Teamsters Union. "Sixty to seventy percent signed pledge cards," according to Teamsters representative James Smith. Some full-time drivers were working shifts as long as twelve hours at rates just a dollar an hour above the minimum wage of $1.65 per hour in 1973. "It's like a slave labor camp," Smith claimed. By 1993, the bus fee per semester had risen to $57. Today, the system runs thirteen routes seven days a week, employs sixty-seven drivers, handles 2.5 million passengers each year, and runs on an annual budget in excess of $2 million. Most importantly, it transformed student housing well away from the campus since students could board a bus to apartment complexes in any area of the city and not have a parking problem on campus.

From Northern's earliest days, DeKalb residents have provided off-campus housing for students. At the beginning of the twentieth century, large homes near the east edge of campus became student rooming houses. In the 1960s, apartment living grew to become an alternative to the dorms even for undergraduates. By the end of the century, students had their pick of large apartment complexes found all over DeKalb. In the 1980s, dorm living had fallen out of favor and most students preferred apartment living. With the end of the concept of in loco parentis, students now saw college as a time to begin to learn to live in the real world. Shopping, cooking, cleaning, and paying the monthly utility bills brought new responsibilities and freedom for many. The bus system enabled most the opportunity to try apartment living in town. The general prosperity of the last two decades of the twentieth century meant most students owned automobiles and brought them to DeKalb. Suburban Estates, James Court, Northern View, Cardinali, and Suburban Apartments housed thousands of students and often brought undergraduates from nearby rural towns into daily contact with the thousands of foreign students who came to Northern for graduate study.

Renting an apartment meant new responsibilities for students who had never signed a lease before, nor were many prepared to carry their own insurance. In the worst apartment complex fire in DeKalb history (right), fire gutted the entire College Square Apartment Saturday night, February 17, 1979. Located in the Greek Row area, College Square was a matched pair of new brick buildings housing nearly four hundred NIU students. When the embers cooled, all were homeless and many lost everything they owned. Only brick pillars stood where fifty-four apartments had housed nearly two hundred students; a sister building had also been severely damaged. The Red Cross, DeKalb churches, university officials, the Salvation Army, and Greek Row organizations combined relief efforts to keep the students going that semester. Happily, there was no loss of life. Mark Fisher, like most, lost everything in the fire. "The insurance cost $25. I didn't buy it when I got my lease," he said. "I don't know anyone who did." Students Paul and Becky Jacob had been married only a year and a half and lost their wedding gifts and pictures in the fire. "The wedding gifts made up most of what we own. I also lost my wedding gown." The DeKalb Fire Department put the loss of building and contents at well over $1 million.

Not all housing in DeKalb was to be found in the brick apartment complexes built in the 1960s and 1970s. Many of the large, older homes in the area just east of the campus became rooming houses, and other, older multiple housing units sometimes converted to student housing. Among the oldest were the Haish Flats (right) on Fisk Avenue just east of the Ellwood House. Jacob Haish built these two-story wood frame units for workers in his barbed wire plant and located the apartments on the north end of his own residential property next to the carriage house and servants' quarters. In the 1950s, these apartments became home to students as enrollments soared and housing came to be in short supply. Located just a few blocks east of the campus and priced at the lower end of rental housing, the Haish Flats proved very attractive to students who wanted more than a room and did not want to stay in the dormitories. They also brought students into a working class residential area and remain today a rental option for both students and DeKalb residents.

Until the commercial development of West Lincoln Highway in the 1960s and the Sycamore Road corridor in the 1970s, students focused on downtown DeKalb for shopping, entertainment, and services. Saloons and taverns, traditionally a mainstay of student entertainment, have been an important part of the downtown scene for over a century.

Jake Crawford's Cigar Store, 1897

While alcohol and tobacco would not have been found on Northern's campus or in the rooms of its students in 1900, the men who worked in the wire mills kept the taverns and tobacco shops on the east end of town in business. A century later, the retail stores on the west end of Main Street (Lincoln Highway) continue to focus on the student trade, and those on the east end market more toward town residents. In 1899, the tight conduct codes in force at the time meant no student would have dared to drink or smoke. In fact, President Cook expelled one student for "rude and profane language at the train station," according to the letter he sent to her parents.

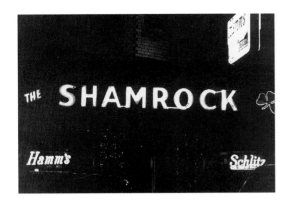

Pour Pat's, 1967

Especially in the 1960s, cultural norms and social attitudes changed rapidly on all college campuses. Although one still could not drink legally until age twenty-one, many college students found ways to enjoy a couple of beers, whether in a park or in a local pub. Two of the more favored watering holes in the 1970s were the Shamrock Bar on Lincoln Highway in the middle of downtown and Pour Pat's, a tavern owned by Charles Cunningham at 507 East Lincoln Highway.

East Lincoln Highway remained the center for nightlife in DeKalb from the 1890s forward, and, by the 1970s, the downtown tavern strip had split into predominantly student bars between First and Fourth Streets with town bars from Fifth through Eighth Streets. Closest to campus and student-oriented were The Uprising, the Shamrock, McCabe's Lounge, Andy's Tap, and the Candlelight Inn. Farther east on Lincoln Highway, Bill and Roger's Tap, Twin Tavern, Keith and Ralph's, and Sullivan's Tavern and Liquors catered mostly to longtime DeKalb residents. Several bars and liquor stores eventually opened in the Greek Row area in the 1980s and along West Lincoln Highway near Annie Glidden in the 1990s. The downtown strip still remains a primary focus for students and residents looking to relax and find some nightlife.

Until the building of the multiscreen theaters in Greek Row (Blackhawk Theaters) and on west Lincoln Highway (Carrol's Cinema), the DeKalb and the Egyptian Theaters brought students downtown to see the films of the day. The DeKalb Theater Company built the Egyptian Theater in 1929 (left). Chicago architect Elmer Behrens designed the building heavily influenced by a popular culture phenomenon, the discovery of the tomb of King Tutankhamen in 1923. The Egyptian Revival fad that swept across America in the twenties brought a number of similar theaters in other cities, but this was the only one built in the Midwest. As business moved out to the new multiscreen theaters in town in the 1970s, the Egyptian fell into disuse and disrepair. It was close to meeting its demolition when local resident Barbara Kummerfeldt formed a group called Preserve the Egyptian Theater (PET) that saved the building and eventually restored it. It had closed to the public in 1977, but by 1982, PET had enlisted enough volunteers and secured enough federal grant funding to do the major repair and restoration work needed to ensure its future. Over the next twenty years, the Egyptian Theater became a cultural events center for the city of DeKalb and also provided a performing arts alternative for the university. The local Kishwaukee Symphony Orchestra now calls the theater home. The Egyptian provides an art gallery for local artists to show their work, and it offers a venue for major national touring productions in the performing arts.

Since 1899, Northern students have been coming to downtown DeKalb to shop as well as to entertain themselves. Once again, the 1960s brought cultural change to staid DeKalb as its first (and only) adult bookstore opened between Fifth and Sixth Streets in 1970. The Paperback Grotto soon moved farther west to be closer to the campus and replaced McCabe's Lounge at 157 East Lincoln Highway. There it has remained and is now closing in on its thirty-fifth anniversary, making it one of the longest continuous runs of any of the downtown shops. This picture was taken in 1976.

Directly across the street from the current location of the Paperback Grotto stood DeKalb's first shopping mall. In this picture, the First National Bank building on the southwest corner of Second Street and Lincoln Highway is surrounded by just about everything anyone would need in 1910 when the picture was taken. Arthur F. Flachtemeier took rooms on the second floor for his dental practice, plumber Eber Lake had a shop in the basement, and the DeKalb Expert Cleaners rented space on the south end of the building right next to the DeKalb Public Library. Within the main office of the bank itself you could find real estate agents Edward Johnson, William Hyde, Joseph Piper, and Walter Poust. Albert Hubbard had his office as a justice of the peace; Lewis D. Carbaugh offered auction services and insurance. If you needed to see a lawyer, attorney Henry W. Prentice worked on the second floor above the Bijou Theater and Billiard Parlor. Mosher and Embree Lumber Company provided supplies for those larger home improvement projects. All on one corner downtown. The First National Bank building stands today as a DeKalb Park District anchor in the downtown, promoting tourism, commerce, and local history.

Just a generation earlier, downtown DeKalb took on an air of a county fair when horse sale day came. At left is a photo taken of the north side of the block between Second and Third Streets in 1895, the year DeKalb won the prize of the new normal school to be built in the northern region of the state.

When the new Northern Illinois State Normal School opened its doors in 1899, students found local merchants catering to their interests.

The dirt roads and wooden sidewalks of the early twentieth century required a good deal of care, and still the dirt streets turned to mud with ruts when bad weather arrived. The invention of the automobile brought rapid changes, and within just twenty years, paved streets and sidewalks were becoming common. The Good Roads Movement had one of its most ardent boosters in Samuel Bradt, a prominent DeKalb businessman who became the first commissioner of roads for the state of Illinois. The photo above is looking west from the intersection of Main Street (now Lincoln Highway) and Fourth, just to the west of the railroad crossing.

To keep the old dirt streets in reasonably decent condition, the city used a team of horses with a wooden platform to drag the dirt level once the mud had dried. The one-man road crew here (right) is seen in 1901 at the corner of Fourth and Pine Streets just north of downtown.

castle on a hill

Downtown DeKalb also provided basic services to students, perhaps none more important than the means to get back home for the weekend and vacations. The DeKalb Sycamore Interurban Traction Company once was a primary means of transportation since it took students down to the Chicago North Western station on its route to Sycamore. The rise of the automobile as the basic means of transportation not only spelled the end for the horse and buggy but for the newly established interurban railroads as well. Early in the twentieth century, few people (and no students) owned automobiles. They depended still on the horse and the train to get around. Students, especially, made use of the Chicago North Western and the DeKalb Sycamore Interurban to get to and from the new Normal School. The Interurban connected with the CNW station downtown and then ran west on Lincoln Highway to Normal Road where it turned north and dead-ended at Williston Hall. This photo at top was taken on Main Street (now Lincoln Highway) near the lagoon.

A photograph (bottom) taken in 1908 several miles out Sycamore Road beautifully illustrates the transportation revolution that was fully underway. The horse and carriage, mainstay of the nineteenth century, has pulled off to the side to give way to the new horseless carriage coming down the middle of the road. To the right, a DeKalb Sycamore Interurban electric rail car is about to pass the horseless carriage. But locals, like Americans everywhere, opted for the independence offered by the automobile over the speed and efficiency offered by mass transit. Just ten years later, the Interurban was no longer running, the horse and buggy days were nearly over, and the age of the internal combustion engine had begun.

DeKalb Bus Depot, 1957

Greyhound Bus Depot, 1993

Since most students did not own cars until the 1970s, the loss of the Interurban left only the bus as a choice for those trips home. Northern has always drawn heavily on the region and Chicago for students, so the Greyhound Bus Depot was a frequent port of call over the first half of the twentieth century. One alumna once suggested that to have a truly Northern homecoming one should assemble all the old grads in DeKalb and then ship them home by bus. The Northern Star runs at least one editorial per year decrying "Suitcase U," but nothing can stop the pull of home-cooked meals, a visit to old friends, and free laundry service. The Greyhound Depot has moved around town over the years, even stopping regularly at the Holmes Student Center for a few years in the 1990s. Here (top photo) the depot is seen located on Second Street just south of Lincoln Highway in 1957. By the end of the twentieth century, there was no passenger rail service and no general bus service to DeKalb.

Few things are more important to college students than mail from home, and the DeKalb Postal Service has brought those welcome packages, letters, and checks to every generation of students since the doors opened in 1899. The stately building at First and Main Streets served as home for the DeKalb Post Office from its opening in 1906 until new quarters at Fourth and Grove opened in 1960. The building pictured above fell to the wrecker's ball in 1995 to make way for a new Walgreens Drug Store. Northern's growth in the 1960s necessitated creating its own Postal Services Department on campus, which works closely with the U.S. Postal Service to deliver millions of pieces each year. Today, the DeKalb Post Office is located near Seventh Street on Lincoln Highway, and the second DeKalb Post Office building at Fourth and Grove is a senior citizens center.

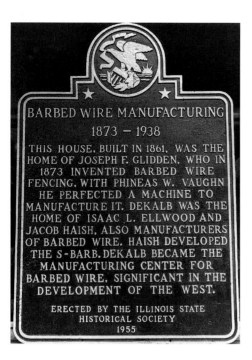

BARBED WIRE MANUFACTURING
1873 – 1938

THIS HOUSE, BUILT IN 1861, WAS THE HOME OF JOSEPH F. GLIDDEN, WHO IN 1873 INVENTED BARBED WIRE FENCING. WITH PHINEAS W. VAUGHN HE PERFECTED A MACHINE TO MANUFACTURE IT. DEKALB WAS THE HOME OF ISAAC L. ELLWOOD AND JACOB HAISH, ALSO MANUFACTURERS OF BARBED WIRE. HAISH DEVELOPED THE S-BARB. DEKALB BECAME THE MANUFACTURING CENTER FOR BARBED WIRE, SIGNIFICANT IN THE DEVELOPMENT OF THE WEST.

ERECTED BY THE ILLINOIS STATE HISTORICAL SOCIETY 1955

DeKalb is known for three things in the state, around the nation, and across the world: Northern Illinois University, hybrid seed corn, and barbed wire. The wire came first. Among historians of the American West, there is consensus that three things forever changed the Trans-Mississippi West in the nineteenth century: the repeating rifle, the railroad, and barbed wire. Local DeKalb hardware merchant Joseph Glidden invented it in DeKalb in 1873, and its rapid spread brought the end of the open range. Today, a historic marker sits on the old Glidden Homestead just west of the Burger King on Lincoln Highway to commemorate the event. Two other individuals important to the manufacture of barbed wire, Isaac Ellwood and Jacob Haish, joined with Glidden in the efforts to secure the new Northern Normal School for DeKalb in 1895. Joseph Glidden invented barbed wire but sold his rights in the patent early on. The homestead remains in place today on West Lincoln Highway and has a support group that is working to restore it to its nineteenth-century look. The brick barn in which Glidden first manufactured the wire that fenced the west is seen on the far right behind the trees in the photo below. This photo, taken in 1955, shows the greenhouses in the center that eventually became the Glidden Campus Florists known to generations of Northern students. Glidden Campus Florists still operates in a building just to the east of the barn today though it is no longer related to the family except in name.

Ellwood House Museum, 1967

Joseph Glidden realized a good deal of profit from the sale of his patent rights but nothing compared to the fortune amassed by Isaac Ellwood, the man to whom he sold half his rights in 1874 for $265. Glidden later sold the other half to an Eastern manufacturer, Washburn and Moen, for $60,000 and a five-cents-per-pound royalty on all wire sold. Ellwood, however, went into the manufacture of wire here in DeKalb and left an estate in the tens of millions when he died in 1910 at the age of seventy-seven. Already in the 1870s, just as he was rising in the manufacture of barbed wire, Ellwood began to purchase land north of downtown and west of First Street. By the spring of 1879 when he began work on what would become the Ellwood Mansion, he owned 1,200 acres. For almost a century, the mansion remained in the family. In the 1960s, Ellwood heirs gave it to the DeKalb Park District, and the DeKalb Fine Arts Association agreed to do the restoration and maintenance needed on the house. Today, it is the historic centerpiece of old town DeKalb.

The Ellwood House may be the best-known historic house in DeKalb, but one of the few longstanding landmarks of the city arrived quite a few years later. "Donna," officially the DeKalb War Memorial Tank, is the property of DeKalb American Legion Post 66 and arrived in 1949 to replace a World War I artillery gun that had been melted down in the World War II effort. The vehicle is technically a Stuart Reconnaissance M-5 that was used in battlefield troop transport in World War II. For over fifty years, "Donna" stood sentinel at the center of town next to the railroad tracks at Fourth Street and Lincoln Highway. When the city created a small park on the corner of First Street and Lincoln Highway in 2001, "Donna" moved to a new home. She is seen here at left in her original setting in October of 1949 just prior to her official dedication as a memorial to those who served in World War I.

More than one thousand men from DeKalb County served in World War I, 763 of them called to serve by the draft that began June 5, 1917, shortly after America entered the war. Even before locals began to enlist or were drafted, war bond rallies served to further the cause of the Allies. Above is a photograph taken in 1917 of a patriotic war bond rally.

The Heroes Return, 1919

The most famous unit from the DeKalb area to serve in the war was Company 129 of the Third Illinois Infantry, part of the Prairie Division that served in France. The 129th suffered 1,445 casualties and captured more than 800 German soldiers. When this unit was called to service at Camp Grant near Rockford, it had more than a few Northern men as members. According to the student newspaper, "When school began in the late summer of 1917, Coach Wirtz discovered we couldn't have a football team this fall." The enlistment of many of Northern's male students had left too few to field a team. "Those who would have been the nucleus around which Chief Wirtz planned to build the team this year are in the army training camps preparing for their journey to Berlin, via France." So the students set a goal of raising $1,500 for a Student Friendship Fund for the forty-seven Northern boys off to the war; they raised $1,863.25. The students and faculty also regularly raised money for the Red Cross. In fact, they decided to forego a yearbook in 1918 and to use the money earmarked for producing the Norther to purchase an ambulance for use in France to help the troops. Each day at the General Exercises, students were reminded of the stakes: "At the front of the auditorium, so elevated that all without effort may see it, hangs our Service Flag. The one hundred twenty-one stars form a shining constellation that no clouds of forgetfulness will ever hide. For every one of them, a student, in the full flush of a splendid young manhood, exchanged the peaceful garb of the scholar for the trim uniform of the soldier." When the Armistice came November 11, 1918, the church bells rang in all the local churches as they did across the country. And when the local doughboys finally returned home, they set up camp just outside of town before returning to Camp Grant to muster out. Northern students went out to welcome the boys back as seen in the photo at left. The Third Illinois Company from DeKalb camp is seen below.

Third Illinois Infantry Camped Near DeKalb Prior to Separation, 1919

Just twenty years later, DeKalb would once again mobilize for war. When Hitler attacked Poland in September of 1939, all Europe stood at the brink of war, and within two years, the entire world was at war. The war would forever change the basic contours of American society with the most profound change taking place in the role of women in the workplace. As millions of men went off to military training, women took their places in the factories, mills, and mines where the war would be won or lost. They quickly learned to operate the machinery, run the assembly lines, and deliver the military hardware essential to the war effort. In DeKalb, Rosie the Riveter learned to work the lathes, drill presses, and milling machines at the Wurlitzer Company. Wurlitzer turned out critical parts for the Army Air Force and built the glider planes used to infiltrate the European theater in the Allied invasion of France in 1944.

Altgeld Hall First Floor Hallway, Honor Roll for World War II

Once again, the men and women of Northern responded to the nation's need by enlisting in substantial numbers. While many local women went into the factories to support the war effort, the men lined up to enlist when America entered the war after December 7, 1941. The war quickly decimated the male student population at Northern, and a number of faculty and staff joined the students at enlistment centers. Hundreds of Northern students enlisted in the first two years of the war, and the total enrollment plummeted 60 percent from 1,008 in 1941 to 435 in 1943. In one week in the spring of 1943, ninety-one Northern men who had enlisted in the reserve were called up, leaving only forty-five men on the campus. The Northern Illinois ran special sections in every issue to try to keep track of former students and also published letters from the troops.

In the last half of the twentieth century, both Sycamore and DeKalb developed an annual festival around which locals could boost the city to the surrounding area. In Sycamore, the Pumpkin Festival became the highlight of the harvest season and an occasion to have a parade, pumpkin-carving competition, street vendors, and a chance to showcase Sycamore for out-of-town guests. Local merchant Wally Thurow explained the origin of the festival: "It all started when I saw a crazy fruit stand with a lot of pumpkins. I bought some and decorated my front lawn with them. Then more and more people started to decorate their front lawns with elaborate displays using pumpkins around Halloween time, until twelve years ago [in 1961] they started a Pumpkin Festival." Thurow's annual pumpkin decoration expanded so much he once had thirty-five pumpkins on his lawn. Some were wired to talk, and others had moving parts. With the help of the Sycamore Lions Club, Thurow made the annual celebration official in 1962. The formal display and competition moved to the front of the Court House. Pumpkin Fest soon attracted the attention of the Chicago television media, and it was not uncommon for over 20,000 people to visit Sycamore over the three-day weekend in the 1980s. DeKalb bicycle dealer Wally Thurow exemplified the civic spirit and fun that marked Pumpkin Fest, and even after he moved to Louisiana, Wally came back each year to ride his old high wheeler in the parade.

DeKalb's answer to Sycamore's Pumpkin Festival was Corn Fest. Corn Fest began as Corn Boil when Del Monte built its DeKalb plant. It became Corn Fest in 1977 when the City of DeKalb under Mayor Judy King began running the annual event through a special committee. It served to welcome students back to DeKalb and to celebrate the role of corn in the county's agriculture and the city's commerce. Carefully setting the dates to correspond with the return of the students, city officials close off the four blocks of downtown between First and Fourth Streets in August each year and throw a giant, three-day block party. Del Monte traditionally supplies a station with free sweet corn, and local volunteers man the giant vats boiling corn fresh from the fields. Since DeKalb was the home of DeKalb AgResearch and corn has been the largest crop in the county for a half-century, Corn Fest was a natural festival for the city. When the sweet corn is ready in mid-August and the students return to DeKalb for the fall semester, downtown streets metamorphose into a combination outdoor shopping mall and weekend carnival. Concert stages, street dances, food booths, carnival games, races, and contests complement the street sales held by downtown merchants. While Del Monte supplies the free sweet corn, local not-for-profit groups supply the rest of the delightful county fair food.

DeKalb's proximity to Chicago has allowed Corn Fest organizers to bring in excellent entertainment talent over the years, and the multiple sound stages offered a chance for every musical taste to be satiated. Here, the Queen of the Blues, Koko Taylor, croons for the 1997 crowd on a stage sponsored by local radio station WDEK-FM.

(Dan Videtich photograph)

As much as DeKalb is known as the home of Northern Illinois University, it is also known as the home of DeKalb Ag Hybrid Seed Corn. That extraordinary story began eighty years ago with two men, Tom Roberts Sr. and Charles L. Gunn. And it was in the midst of the Great Depression that this small company began its journey to a worldwide enterprise. DeKalb Ag traces its roots to the DeKalb County Soil Improvement Association founded in 1912 by Henry H. Parke. Seed corn production and the creation of hybrids began when Charles Gunn arrived in 1917. With the severe droughts and winters of the thirties, specialized seed corn became critical to food production in the Midwest. In 1936, the DeKalb County Soil Improvement Association began to produce seed corn for farmers outside the county. DeKalb Ag's winged ear trademark soon became one of the best recognized across the rural American landscape.

castle on a hill

In this photo, one of the world's pioneers in the creation of hybrids, Charlie Gunn, is seen looking over sample results of lab work and field trials. Gunn literally changed the history of the world with his advances in plant genetics as fewer and fewer acres could feed more and more people. Still today, nearly a century after Roberts and Gunn began to transform corn agriculture, DeKalb County is known for its intense cultivation and extraordinary yields of corn. Virtually all NIU students for the past century have made their way through the tall corn of late August or early September to return to classes each year. In DeKalb County, corn is still king.

In DeKalb County, corn is still king.

chapter seven
TOWN GOWN RELATIONS

Since the invention of the university in the Middle Ages, relations between town and gown have always been both ambivalent and symbiotic. The foundations of Northern Illinois University begin with Clinton Rosette, editor of the *DeKalb Daily Chronicle*. From the very beginning, then, the city of DeKalb and Northern have been in close relationship. A number of northern Illinois cities competed to have the Illinois Legislature site a new normal school in their community, but the strong efforts of Rosette, Isaac Ellwood, Joseph Glidden, and Jacob Haish—prominent town residents all—won the prize for DeKalb.

A celebration in October of 1895 brought a crowd of thirty thousand to DeKalb for groundbreaking ceremonies that included food, music, speeches, a parade, and fireworks. The impact of such a huge gathering on local businesses, roads, and accommodations set the foundation for town gown relations. There would be enormous economic consequences from a school in DeKalb. Equally important, the social and cultural life of DeKalb would change, the composition of the residents would change, and the local public school system would become a citywide laboratory for teaching the teachers.

Both natural and created boundaries separate town and gown in DeKalb. For a century, the Kishwaukee River and Lincoln Highway have been the points at which town and gown meet. The land for the central campus was a gift to the state by Joseph Glidden, who donated sixty-three acres bordering the river and the main road.

DeKalb residents planned a special, two-day festival called Crimson Days to celebrate Northern's opening to students. September 21 and 22 in 1899 brought parades, picnics, outdoor entertainment, food booths, fireworks, and local politicians out to party. Despite cool temperatures and rain, all of the events took place, including the parade. The festooned horse and buggy above was part of that parade.

Crimson Days set a precedent for what would, in later years, become the largest town gown party of the year, homecoming. In the early years, Northern's homecomings were small simply because there were not yet many alumni. But that would change over time, and the annual fall ritual of a homecoming weekend featured a parade on Lincoln Highway and a Saturday afternoon football game usually followed by a dance and plenty of smaller parties.

Homecoming often brought out the best in town gown cooperation. Local merchants benefited from increased business, and they often sponsored floats and special events, which students wanted. Here the Golden Anniversary Homecoming Parade of 1949 made its way through the heart of downtown DeKalb on Lincoln Highway.

Student interest in the parades peaked in the fifties. The parade would continue to be a part of homecoming until the nineties, but the student activism of the sixties soon brought new issues to the fore for many students. Civil rights, student rights, and antiwar movements visited the Northern campus and brought a new tension to town gown relations.

Another good example of the many small ways town and gown complement each other is the annual opening of the university's lagoon as the primary skating rink for DeKalb. For two or three months each winter, students from Northern share the pond with the skaters who live in DeKalb and have no other place to skate.

Cooperation and mutual benefit is most often the case in the town gown relationship but not always. By its very nature, the university brings to DeKalb young people who often want to challenge the status quo and push the social bounds and who bring new cultures into the community.

Twenty years ago, a local resident and NIU librarian, Eileen Dubin, directed a "Town Gown Oral History" project. Interviewers talked with forty-seven prominent DeKalb people about the relationships between Northern and DeKalb in the post–World War II era. These interviews cover a broad range of subjects and are now available for research use in the university's Regional History Center. One of the hottest topics discussed in these interviews was the student protest movement of the 1960s. Student activism rose to unprecedented heights on the NIU campus in the sixties as it did on many American campuses, and the attendant protest marches marked a new era in town gown relations.

The spring of 1970 brought the period of greatest tension and conflict to the relations between students and DeKalb residents. Throughout the 1960s, students had become more and more involved in public demonstrations supporting civil rights and against the growing war in Southeast Asia. One warm night in May 1970, ten years of building tension boiled over. Northern President Rhoten Smith sat in the middle of the Lincoln Highway Bridge (above) that night to keep the students on their side as they faced police, National Guard, and hostile town residents. Smith averted a potential disaster, but this showdown and the violence of the days surrounding it marked the peak of tension between town and gown over the past century.

Town gown relations are as obvious as the university's dependence on DeKalb for fire protection, water supply, sanitary sewers, and access roads. In turn, DeKalb relies on the fees and revenue received for these services, and profits from the huge economic engine driven by staff salaries and student spending. There are also hidden, complex, and sensitive issues such as cultural conflicts in off-campus housing, mass transit on and off campus, and the role students play in town politics.

In 1899, Alice Crosby, a Northern student, said, "Expressions of welcome from the people of DeKalb have been heard on every hand and are very gratifying to us." Crosby, first editor of the student newspaper, concluded that "we shall long remember our kindly reception by DeKalb's people, and we hope to be able to bring something into the community life that shall give expression to our appreciation of their thoughtfulness."

A well-known legend has it that local folks put a dam on the Kishwaukee River and benefited from a heavy rain the night before the legislative site selection committee visited DeKalb looking for a place to locate a Northern Illinois Normal School in 1895.

For the past century, both Northern and the DeKalb community have made the most of this modest little stream flowing through town. It is one of the few in North America that flows from south to north. The name, Kishwaukee, comes from the Potawatomi word for the sycamore, or cottonwood, tree.

The lagoon just west of the river took shape early in Northern's history. The lagoon began as a shallow mud hole that filled with water during heavy spring rains. Already in the fall of 1905, Northern groundskeeper W. C. Claybaugh laid out a landscape project that would "involve the moving of twenty-five thousand cubic yards of earth." Terraces and gardens would greet visitors coming into the campus from the east and south, and, said Claybaugh, "the old ice pond will be greatly enlarged and the present water level raised about six feet."

Two years later, Frank Balthis noted, "perhaps no single feature of the campus has given more satisfaction—especially to the children since skating began—than the lake, which was completed in November [1907]." Through extensive excavation, Balthis added, the pond was now seven acres and, even better, "a series of pools and miniature waterfalls" marked the connection through a small dam to the river.

The Kishwaukee River then, as now, often swelled with heavy rains and flooded in the spring. Since all students lived in town, they daily walked across the bridges and came to appreciate the river. To give the lagoon character, Claybaugh and Balthis laid out an irregular shoreline replete with a small island separated from the shore by twenty feet. Balthis, a botanist, then planted the hundreds of plants and trees that surrounded the river and lagoon banks, and he established a series of gardens on the multiple terraces that led the way to the Castle on the Hill.

The Great Depression in the 1930s brought the next major work on the lagoon. The Civil Works Administration undertook as its most far-reaching project in the county, rebuilding and landscaping the lagoon area. Work began in 1934 and provided jobs for both students and unemployed people in town. This CWA effort created a new Castle Drive and the triple-arched bridge just to the north of the lagoon. The work force averaged fifty laborers over two years of work and peaked at providing employment for 167.

The Works Progress Administration provided complementary work in the dredging of the lagoon. Using local farmers and their teams of horses, the WPA project drained the south end and dug it deeper. The north end followed, and finally, in the fall of 1936, both projects had been completed.

Over the past century, the Kishwaukee River and the lagoon have provided more enjoyment than one can imagine for such unpretentious bodies of water. Many children have wet their first fishing line in the lagoon, the island has seen weddings, and an Olympic Gold Medal skater trained on the bumpy ice. The surrounding area has been the stage for Shakespeare on the lawn and, more recently, been home to Jazz in the Night. For decades, spring commencement took place outdoors at the lagoon. As the top picture shows, the lagoon also provided ice for DeKalb homes and businesses in the early part of the century.

1954 Flood

The Kishwaukee River seems to flood at least once every decade. The most memorable will be debated between the older and younger generations: Was it the flood of 1954? Was it the flood in the summer of 1978? Or the one caused by the nine inches of rain that fell July 17–18 in 1996? The U.S. Army Corps of Engineers came in to build the levees and somewhat straighten the river in the 1950s, but Mother Nature, in the end, is always stronger.

Watson Crick, the small stream that flows across the campus into the lagoon, is named for Nobel Prize winners James D. Watson and Francis H. Crick; they developed the model for DNA structure. As part of the Centennial Celebration, the university improved and restored the area. New bridges cross Watson Crick, the Castle Drive Gates have been restored, and major efforts to improve campus drainage to avoid future floods have been completed.

As modest as the Kishwaukee River and the NIU Lagoon are, there are few spots that are more important to the history of both town and gown over the past century. As Frank Balthis said nearly a century ago, "perhaps no single feature of the campus has given more satisfaction." They have served both as a friendly fence and a bridge between town and gown. The NIU president's house also sits on the banks of the Kishwaukee in the middle of town just off Sycamore Road. Northern's Board of Regents purchased the house from President Rhoten Smith in 1971 when he left the university. The original president's house on College Avenue had been sold in 1921 upon President Cook's retirement. His successor, J. Stanley Brown, chose to live in an apartment created on the first floor of Williston Hall "to accommodate his invalid wife." For fifty years, Northern did not provide a home for the president.

An example of the best of town gown cooperation is the blacktop bike and walking path that winds its way along the west bank of the Kishwaukee from the far south side of DeKalb, through the NIU campus, and all the way to the far north side of DeKalb. There it connects with another bike path that takes riders through Sycamore and then on to St. Charles. A local Kiwanis group teamed with Northern to lay down the first section of this path from Lincoln Highway across the campus to First Street. For thirty years, the bike path has provided a safe place for joggers and bicyclists and a convenient means for students and staff to get to campus without driving or taking the bus.

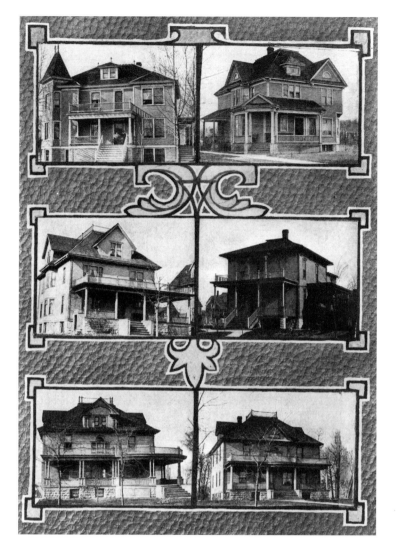

When Northern opened its doors in 1899, local residents quickly expanded their homes to provide both housing and meals for the 120 students who enrolled. For nearly twenty years, these large homes just east of the Kishwaukee River provided the "clubs" in which students stayed and in which they made a home away from home. The area is still predominantly student housing.

Half a dozen large homes built in the Augusta and College Streets neighborhood became rooming houses the students called clubs. Named after the people who owned and lived in them, the Hurt Club, the Kilmer Club, and the Tudor Club became institutions in their own right. Each had pride, unity, and social programs similar to the social sororities that came later.

There were all-male clubs as well, but fewer of them since 70 percent of the students were female in the early decades. Reports on activities in the clubs regularly found their way onto the social page of the student newspaper, the Northern Illinois.

Three of the structures pictured here—the Shafer (top left), the Benson (middle left), and the Rickard (bottom left)—still house students today. When the owner of the residence would change so would the name of the club.

These homeowners also supplied meals for the residents and some in loco parentis supervision as well as personal counseling. Mary and Porter Shafer built the Shafer House in 1900 at 247 West Locust (Park and Locust), and it enjoyed the longest life of all the clubs, fifty-seven years. While the capacity for roomers was seventeen, Mrs. Shafer often fed as many as one hundred for lunch in the early days. After her death, the family established a scholarship at Northern in her name.

The going rate for a room with meals was about $4.00 a week while school was in session. Homeowners did advertise and compete much as apartment complexes do today. One ad in the local paper in 1900 offered "excellent meals and good rooms for $3.50 and $4.00 per week at Mrs. Chesebro's, 506 South Third Street." A bit farther to walk in the winter, but the price and the food made it worth the walk.

The student newspaper, a monthly publication in those first years, carried social notes from the clubs in each edition. Here we see four students posed in front of Dadd's House in 1906. They had returned from church and were enjoying a light lunch on the front lawn while studying for the next day's classes.

While the clubs did compete for residents, they also helped each other out when necessary. When "one of the Benson children came down with a light attack of diphtheria, November 4, [1906,]…the Benson Club was quarantined for about ten days and the roomers and boarders had to seek accommodation elsewhere, temporarily. Most of them went to the Tudor Club," reported the student newspaper.

Most of the clubs also offered lunch for day students who came to campus early each morning but could make it home each night to surrounding communities. With no fast food and few restaurants, commuter students welcomed these home-cooked lunches.

One consequence of the influx of resident students was the growth of the support businesses and none more so than local food providers. Even with meals furnished, students were forever looking for some social activities including food and partying. On a birthday or a holiday or perhaps just to have some fun, women in the clubs would throw a "spread." That is, they would go down to the local grocer and stuff a large picnic basket full of goodies to share with people in the house.

A typical item run in the student newspaper would report: "The student teachers at the Shafer Club entertained their critics at dinner Sunday, December eighteenth [1910]. The table was daintily decorated with holiday sprays. After dinner the Misses Hogan and Suit favored the party with some beautiful selections on the piano." One of the places students frequented to stock up for the parties was the Lon Smith Meat Market. The photo below is Smith's market prepared for the Christmas season of 1905.

Nancy Fike's Room, 1907

Today, of course, the tens of thousands of students who live and shop in DeKalb bring tens of millions of dollars into the local economy and are central to it. Even rather minor drops in enrollment ripple through the housing and food markets with substantial impact. And there are still students living in the private homes of residents throughout DeKalb.

Ever since Williston Hall opened to students in 1915, Northern has itself provided dormitory and food services for most residential students. A century later, there are more commuters than ever, but local business still thrives on the trade brought in by students. For the most part, it has been an amicable and pleasant relationship for both the students and those who provide them housing. The foundation for that relationship was laid in the clubs along the Kishwaukee a hundred years ago.

One of the three conditions that Northern trustees met to get John Williston Cook to lead the new Northern Illinois Normal was the opportunity to use the DeKalb public schools as a practice laboratory for students. The trustees convinced the good citizens of DeKalb to open their local schools as a training ground for Northern's faculty and students. In 1911, Northern opened the McMurry Training School as the second building on campus, and it functioned as an integral part of the local school system. A devastating fire (bottom left) destroyed one of DeKalb's elementary schools on January 27, 1902. Janitor Anthony Nelson discovered an overheated furnace in flames when he made the morning rounds to check temperatures around 8:45 a.m. All the children left the building within five minutes, so there were no injuries, but within two hours, the building stood in ruins.

The $40,000 fire destroyed the building and all its contents. Wooden ventilator shafts had quickly spread the fire through the building, and the cold, windy day fed the fire from without. It was the worst public building fire in DeKalb history.

Northern faculty and students came to the assistance of local school officials in finding ways to fit the displaced students into the remaining facilities.

Northern's first history professor, Edward Carlton Page (left), arrived on the Northern campus in the fall of 1899, and he, too, wanted to enrich the elementary classrooms in DeKalb. He began to talk with DeKalb residents about building a collection of historical materials on the campus that could be used to teach American history in local classrooms.

Page accumulated local historical artifacts that he used in his own teaching and soon developed a collection large enough to create a small museum in Altgeld Hall. In 1912, that museum became reality and was opened to the residents and schoolchildren of the city.

"Our own museum is not quite three years old," Page noted in 1915, "yet we have assembled about two thousand separate items besides a collection of two thousand Indian relics donated by one of our citizens." His most important goal, Page added, was "taking the objects into the classroom."

Page died in 1929, but his partnership with town residents in preserving local history lived on. While the remnants of the Page collection are still maintained as an active museum collection at Northern, the emphasis over the past forty years has been to preserve the historical records of both the university and DeKalb.

Shown in the picture here are a dozen items from the Page Collection taken out into the schools to show the various kinds of lighting common in the eighteenth and nineteenth centuries. The advent of gas lighting in the 1890s and electric light at the beginning of the twentieth century had begun to revolutionize daily life for millions. The new types of lighting made night work, including homework, much easier and safer.

Northern faculty offered expertise and help in the community well beyond the public schools. One of the more spectacular examples in the earliest years was the discovery of mastodon bones on Jacob Hochstrasser's farm just east of DeKalb. The September 17, 1907, headline in the DeKalb Chronicle proudly proclaimed "DeKalb to Have a Mastodon." "Much interest has been aroused in DeKalb and vicinity by the recent discovery of a mastodon on the farm of Mr. Hochstrasser, three miles south of Maple Park. . . . A movement is already underfoot to procure this prehistoric giant by popular subscription and bring it to DeKalb to be placed in the museum of the Northern Illinois State Normal." President Cook and biology professor Fred Charles led the local contingent out to the Hochstrasser farm to oversee the dig and assess the find.

In this picture, President John Williston Cook stands at the far right holding up two of the lower leg bones. In December of 1906, Hochstrasser had begun to excavate a small drainage ditch in a low-lying area. On April 29, 1907, the farmer discovered an upper tooth from a mastodon. In late May, he found two more teeth and part of a skull that had been broken and uncovered by the scoop. When school convened in September, Professor Charles went out to the field on Saturday, September 14, and the digging began in earnest. Local newspaperman and avid photographer Herbert Wells Fay took these pictures. Today, the bones reside at the Smithsonian Museum of Natural History in Washington, D.C., and are under the control of the Department of Paleobiology.

The town gown partnership begun by professor of history Edward Page in 1899 has blossomed into a resource he would be proud of a century later. The Hochstrasser dig is just one of many stories where Northern and the community have worked together over the past one hundred years to create a permanent legacy for future generations.

Here at left, Jacob Hochstrasser's son-in-law is shown posing with the excavated mastodon leg bones.

*Mathematics professor Swen Franklin
Parson also made a contribution to town
life that endures to this day. Among
those President Cook considered critical
to the success of the Northern Normal
School was Swedish-born mathematics
professor, Swen Franklin Parson. A
Cook confidante and protégé, Parson
had been director of the practice teaching
school in Bloomington. Of the fifteen
original Northern faculty members,
Parson remained on staff the longest
until his retirement in 1935.*

*Parson was a bibliophile and joined the DeKalb Public Library Board in 1906. He remained a member of the board until his death in 1949 and chaired
the board for forty years.*

*The DeKalb Chronicle Building at First and Main Streets housed the DeKalb Public Library as seen in the top photo. It had been located just south of
Main Street on Second Street behind the bank building before moving to the Chronicle Building. Barbed wire magnate and public philanthropist Jacob
Haish donated the funds necessary to build the current building at the corner of Third and Oak that opened February 15, 1931.*

*The Haish Library benefited from Parson's leadership and from his commitment to the highest standards in building a library collection. For his efforts, the
Illinois Library Association awarded its Distinguished Service Award posthumously to Parson in November 1949, shortly after his death. It was also in
1949 that work on Northern's new campus library had begun, and Northern, too, chose to honor Parson's long and illustrious career by naming the new
library for him (above).*

The silent Influence of Books is a Mighty Power in the World ▮▮ and there is a Joy in Reading them Known Only to those who Read them with Desire and Enthusiasm ▮▮ Silent Passive and Noiseless, though they be They yet set in Action countless Multitudes and Change the Order of Nations

Giles

Architect C. Herrick Hammond's traditional Gothic architecture brought beauty to the first major library facility on the campus. With its vaulted ceilings, leaded glass windows, and exterior stonework, Swen Parson Hall remains one of the gems on the central campus. This photo captures Parson's credo inscribed over the circulation desk in the main lobby: "The silent influence of books is a mighty power in the world. . . ."

Swen Parson was a man with insatiable curiosity, extraordinary vision, and an unbounded willingness to serve. In retirement, he traveled all over the world, and his unpublished autobiography is truly a testament to a life dedicated to learning. After he retired, Parson took a six-month trip around the world at the age of seventy-six. He notes in his diary for February 10, 1937:

> We located at Mt. Everest Hotel, Darjeeling, after driving from Siliguri 56 miles, 50 of which are a steep mountain climb. Our elevation was 7,000 feet, a mere nothing compared to the snow-clad Himalayas in sight toward the north. The clouds hung over them so that we could not see the top. The city of Darjeeling is built on a hillside. The streets wind about at different levels. Sometimes one has to climb long stairs to get to the next street. Mt. Everest Hotel contained no central heating plant. The slight cold I caught on the sleeper did not improve and I feared that my vaccination would not help much in getting rid of it. Therefore I decided to cut out the rickshaw ride scheduled for the afternoon and sleep something or other off.

Such is the stuff of which legends are made and for whom buildings are named. Swen Parson Hall on the NIU campus now serves as the home of several administrative offices and the College of Law.

While students and faculty may have the most obvious impact on the relations between town and gown, there are also powerful, unseen forces that daily affect both parties in the relationship. Nowhere is this more the case than in the utilities essential to running both the city and the university. Each year, Northern Illinois University relies on the city of DeKalb for its water, its fire protection services, and for sanitary sewers. For these services, the university pays the city approximately $1 million.

The university also relies on outside governments and private utilities for access roads, natural gas, electricity, and television cable service. Northern's impact on the local and regional economy for basic infrastructure and utilities is substantial since these bills total more than $6 million a year. A century ago, Northern began life far more independent than it is today. Even then, it relied on the city for some basic services such as police, fire, water, and the newly invented telephone.

Altgeld Hall was the only building on campus when Northern opened in 1899 and, being constructed of stone, concrete, and marble, was highly fire resistant. Nonetheless, its height, size, and distance from a good water source posed new problems for the DeKalb Fire Department. The picture above was taken in front of Altgeld and published in the first student yearbook.

DeKalb Electric Light, 1894

The DeKalb Fire Department, organized in the 1870s, had three companies under the direction of Marshal William H. Miller in 1899. All the equipment was horse-drawn; the first mechanized fire truck did not arrive until 1916, the year after Williston Hall opened as Northern's first dormitory. The advent of the high-rise dorms on the west campus in the early 1960s also required the purchase of special equipment to reach the upper floors in an emergency. Equipment purchased in part with fees received for fire protection from Northern also improved town protection.

Today, Northern relies on large public utilities for its energy supplies of gas and electricity. A century ago, it was more self-sufficient. Local businessmen John W. Glidden and Samuel E. Bradt had established the DeKalb Electric Company in the early 1890s. But architect Charles Brush had designed a self-sufficient building. A large dynamo built into Altgeld Hall provided the electricity needed to power the hundreds of lights in the large auditorium.

Electric lighting was still new in 1899 and had not supplanted gas lighting in most public places. The Altgeld auditorium was on the leading edge of technology for its day. Students and visitors stood in awe when the 500 bulbs transformed the darkness into light. The main dynamo also provided power to the 300 sixteen-candlepower lights throughout the rest of the building and the fans used to circulate air through it.

Today, Northern gets all its electrical power from the outside and provides most of its own telecommunications infrastructure. In 1899, it provided all its own electrical power but relied on the DeKalb Telephone Company for its telecommunications.

This picture below, taken in 1900, shows the main office and switchboard for the telephone company. Pictured left to right: Cora Tudor, operator; Belle Williams, operator; [unidentified] head lineman; Glen Reynolds, manager; Delia Lovelle, long distance; Florence Herrick, chief operator. A chalkboard on the back wall (center) recorded the names and numbers of new customers.

In 1899, students did not have individual phone service, of course, nor did faculty have individual phones in their offices. Telecommunications a century later now encompass everything from mobile cell phones to Internet access and video transmission through satellite up and down links. While the university does work closely with major private providers of telecommunications services, it does much on its own.

Northern's dependence on outside providers for primary utility services has brought many jobs into the community and the region. When the students are in residence, the demand for water and for sanitary sewage treatment is almost equal to the city outside the campus. Many local residents also found jobs supplying the basic services the campus requires to function.

NIU's impact on DeKalb streets and roads is also significant. Students passed a referendum in 1971 to establish a bus system to travel throughout the city. Although students paid for the system in full, the buses took a very heavy toll on city streets. Street repair and rebuilding required over the next several decades because of the bus traffic was expensive. At the same time, the buses allowed students to rent apartments far from campus and brought shoppers into many stores and businesses that profited from the system. And DeKalb residents did have access to mass transit on a fee-for-service basis.

There are areas of shared or cooperative services where town and gown have pooled resources. The rebuilding of Lucinda Avenue through the heart of the campus area is one example. The cooperation of DeKalb and NIU Police Departments is another. At other times, the university and town officials have disagreed. The collection of sales tax on Holmes Student Center hotel rooms is an example where town and gown clashed.

The university puts a strain on local resources at times, but, overall, the city benefits from the revenues received from the university. Each day, for tens of thousands of people both on the campus and off, the water flows, the lights go on, police provide security, computers flash out onto the Internet, the buses roll, and the fire department is ready for emergencies. It is a vast, complex, and cooperative effort of town and gown to provide the basic infrastructure essential to life in DeKalb. It is a partnership that serves both town and gown well and took a century to build. Today, one of the first sentinels seen on the roads leading into DeKalb is the large water tower on the west edge of the campus announcing DeKalb as the "Home of the Huskies."

DeKalb Water Towers, 1894 and 1997 (bottom)

castle on a hill

One of the primary intersects of town and gown is in the daily commerce the students bring to the shops and businesses of DeKalb. For the most part, that relationship has been a good one, but, on occasion, a local business clashes with the students who are the customers. One important example of that came to downtown DeKalb in the fall of 1946.

The flood of World War II veterans returning home in 1945 armed with the G.I. Bill forever changed college campuses across America. Northern was no exception. Enrollment at Northern swelled from 581 in 1945 to 1,442 in 1946 and hit 2,073 in 1949, an increase of 400 percent in three years.

The returning veterans had paid a high price to secure freedom for their country, and the U.S. government encouraged as many as possible to get a higher education through the G.I. Bill. The men and women who flooded college campuses were often quite different than those who had been enrolled in the prewar years. They were older, more mature, highly motivated, and eager to move quickly back into civilian life. To the small bucolic Northern campus, they brought a revolution. Part of that revolution was the arrival of new ethnicity and new cultures.

While there had been students from Asian, African American, and Hispanic cultures at Northern through its first forty-five years, they were few. They also were too often not welcomed in DeKalb by some of the town residents. In 1946, Northern students challenged that resistance, and the World War II vets became the catalyst for DeKalb's first civil rights protest.

At the center of this change was an extraordinarily talented, unassuming Navy veteran, Ernest "Bumpy" Smith. Bumpy, a star on the Northern track team is shown above in 1948 between his teammates Mickey McMillian (left) and Jay Gulotte (right). Smith starred on the track team, chaired the American Veterans Committee, and was president of the Social Science Club; also, his peers elected him president of the senior class in the fall of 1948.

Smith, a native of Chicago Heights, went into the U.S. Navy straight out of high school in 1943. After completing boot camp at Great Lakes Naval Training Station, Bumpy shipped west to San Francisco, and the Navy then posted him to the South Pacific theater. When the war had ended, Smith came to Northern in 1946 to pursue a college education. Like many of his peers, he had survived the Great Depression and the war and now looked forward to a future full of promise.

Students had long favored the Log Cabin Restaurant on Lincoln Highway, and, in the fall of 1946, it was THE place to hang out. Bumpy Smith soon found out he was not welcome there.

"I used to go down there with guys from my hometown for lunch," Smith remembers. "And I noticed . . . we'd be the last to be waited on. And these guys, they didn't know what the hell was going on. I knew what was going on. Finally, they told me not to come back to that place." When some of Smith's friends, also veterans, heard, according to Smith, they were incensed. "They called this assembly to do something about this discrimination. . . . That auditorium was packed. There wasn't one seat vacant."

The students decided a boycott was in order and instituted it against two downtown restaurants that, according to the student newspaper, "refused to seat Negroes in their places of business." One of Smith's friends, Jack Frooman, chaired the Veterans Committee, and he led the students to vote the boycott. Frooman then worked with Professor Charles Howell from the social sciences department to negotiate with the restaurant owners. Howell at the time served on the Illinois Governor's Committee on Inter-Racial Relations.

After several meetings, the owners decided retreat was the better part of valor and changed policies to allow anyone to eat in their restaurants. Smith, for one, appreciated the peer support: "That boycott was successful. And finally Howell, Dr. Howell, did some negotiating and ended it. But the students really rallied around me in that particular instance. It was something to behold."

Today, Smith resides in a Detroit suburb, retired from a long and successful teaching career. He still has a deep appreciation for his alma mater. Like Rosa Parks, Bumpy Smith does not see himself as a pioneer or a local hero for what happened a half-century ago. Smith and his friends did change the course of town gown relations and set a course that still helps to shape the local environment.

On October 23, 1948, the Log Cabin Restaurant burned in a major fire, a fire not related to its history as the place that gave birth to civil rights in DeKalb over a half-century ago.

Generally, of course, businesses downtown catered to students and sought to give the customer what he or she needed. Until the creation of the University Bookstore and the Village Commons Bookstore in the late sixties, there was just one place to get the books you needed for class: Secor's Drug Store in downtown DeKalb. This photo is from the spring of 1962.

Just twenty-five years after that first civil rights protest had challenged local residents to change the established order, a more virulent era of protests arrived in DeKalb.

The growing antiwar movement on American campuses built to a crescendo on May 4, 1970, when Ohio National Guardsmen shot and killed four students on the Kent State campus. The fury the Kent killings generated quickly built into a fire on the NIU campus that led to the worst town gown relations of the past century.

On the Northern campus, a number of hot issues began to meld into the student anger that underwrote two weeks of marches, confrontation, and violence in May 1970. The university's participation in the ROTC program came to a vote, the attempt to initiate a Police Science Program at Northern failed, and the killing of two African American students at Jackson State a week after the Kent State violence brought the cauldron to a boil.

Antiwar and civil rights advocates on the NIU campus had been active for several years and had led marches to support their causes. The killing of students in Kent, Ohio, and Augusta, Mississippi, in the first two weeks of May brought students out by the thousands for the first time in DeKalb.

The Vietnam War and the acceleration of the draft in the late 1960s swept students out of college classrooms and into protest marches on many campuses across the country. The disproportionate numbers of African Americans being drafted and killed in the war began a confluence of the civil rights movement with the antiwar movement. As events in Ohio and Mississippi seemed to show, counterviolence against student protest struck as easily at historically black colleges as at predominantly white schools.

In the wake of the Kent State violence on May 4, Northern president Rhoten Smith called for a two-day moratorium on classes beginning May 7. "In this situation," said Smith, "I believe a period of meditation, reflection, and self-examination for the university is very much in order." Many students, faculty, and DeKalb residents did not agree with Smith's canceling classes.

Almost daily protest marches soon swelled in size until over 8,000 turned out one night. Isolated incidents of rock throwing and window breaking marred some of the marches and led to the arrest of over thirty students by local police.

Two weeks after Kent State, the Jackson State killings caused Smith to call a second two-day moratorium for May 18 and 19. Civil rights activist Father James Groppi spoke on the night of May 18,

igniting another protest. This time, some in the crowd began to throw rocks as the crowd moved across the campus toward downtown DeKalb. By midnight, protesting students occupied the bridge across Lincoln Highway at the lagoon.

Waiting for the crowd on the other side of the bridge were NIU Police, DeKalb Police, Illinois State Police, and the DeKalb County Sheriff's Deputies. The Illinois National Guard remained in reserve at the Sycamore Armory. Rumors that local business people were waiting inside their shops downtown to greet marauding students with loaded weapons added tension to the standoff.

In an attempt to defuse this confrontation between town and gown, President Rhoten Smith came out to join the students on the bridge and sat down with his NIU baseball cap on. For three hours, neither side moved. Then, just after three o'clock in the morning, the police moved in with gas and clubs to clear the highway of students. Fortunately, there were no serious injuries though several dozen more students were arrested and property damage on campus went into the tens of thousands of dollars.

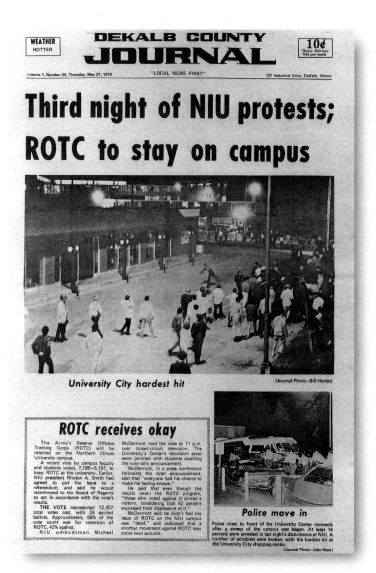

WEATHER HOTTER

DEKALB COUNTY JOURNAL

10¢ Home Delivery 60¢ per week

Volume 1, Number 24, Thursday, May 21, 1970   "LOCAL NEWS FIRST"   121 Industrial Drive, DeKalb, Illinois

Third night of NIU protests; ROTC to stay on campus

University City hardest hit

(Journal Photo—Bill Hartin)

ROTC receives okay

The Army's Reserve Officers Training Corps (ROTC) will be retained on the Northern Illinois University campus.

A record vote by campus faculty and students voted, 7,186–5,197, to keep ROTC at the university. Earlier, NIU president Rhoten A. Smith had agreed to put the issue to a referendum, and said he would recommend to the Board of Regents to act in accordance with the vote's results.

THE VOTE represented 12,407 total votes cast, with 24 spoiled ballots. Approximately 58% of the vote count was for retention of ROTC, 42% against.

NIU ombudsman Michael McDermott read the vote at 11 p.m. over closed-circuit television. The University's Center's television areas were jammed with students awaiting the vote tally announcement.

McDermott, in a press conference following the total announcement, said that "everyone had his chance to make his feeling known."

He said that even though the results retain the ROTC program, "those who voted against it scored a victory, considering that 42 percent expressed their displeasure at it."

McDermott said he didn't feel the issue of ROTC on the NIU campus was "dead," and indicated that a another movement against ROTC may come next autumn.

Police move in

Police mass in front of the University Center moments after a sweep of the campus was begun. At least 14 persons were arrested in last night's disturbance at NIU. A number of windows were broken, with the hardest hit at the University City shopping center.

(Journal Photo—John Mark)

The following night was the end of two weeks of marches and violence as students ranged west on Lincoln Highway and caused significant property damage to stores in University City. In the two weeks, over 150 students were arrested and a lot of windows broken both on and off campus. Students also burned several university vehicles in the nightly raids.

Northern housing director Don Buckner remembered those weeks as a time that "really ignited the city people against the university. Not understanding." Many did not think the president had taken a tough enough stand. There were more than a few, according to Buckner, who thought "we should be bashing their heads in rather than talking with them or sitting down in that baseball cap."

A number of the students present at the disturbances later said that one major problem was the deputizing of civilians who did want to bash a few heads. Some of these temporary deputies were part of the police lines around the dorms on the west campus and did go into the dorms to drag people out. While thirty years have calmed nerves on both sides of the bridge, there are still some very passionate views on campus and in town about the two weeks in May 1970.

For the most part, town and gown cooperate to the benefit of both sides. One example is the music and art that the university brings into the community. Each year, NIU's School of Music provides over one hundred free recitals and concerts open to the public. The fine and performing arts scene in DeKalb thrives on the talents of both students and faculty and enriches town culture. The music is not always just on the campus. If you look closely, you will find the town gown music relationship in almost every church, school, and musical organization in DeKalb.

For centuries, it has been the custom in university towns for music faculty to work in the local churches. This relationship gives the performing artist a venue, it affords a high quality of music for worshipers, and it offers conductors and composers a chance to work with a choir.

As has been the case for a hundred years, musical talent from Northern moves out into the community and can be heard in many churches each week. Choir directors, organists, and student or faculty soloists may be found in churches and organizations throughout the community. Town residents who have no affiliation with Northern are found at the many concerts and recitals given on campus each year. The Steel Drum Band plays to a packed audience, as does the NIU Philharmonic when it brings in children for the annual Halloween Concert.

The NIU Community School of Music offers lessons to children throughout the DeKalb community at low cost to supplement the music curriculum offered in area public schools. Aspiring violinist Ian Marsden (right) was part of the Suzuki teaching program within the Community School of Music. Suzuki builds a partnership of parent, student, and teacher in bringing young children into the world of classical music. Over the years, thousands of children have taken lessons through this program, and some of them have gone on to careers in music.

Crewcuts Concert, 1956

The university also offers opportunities to see popular performers and national speakers who would not ever play in a town like DeKalb except for the university's presence. Hal Holbrook, Eleanor Roosevelt, Wynton Marsalis, Bill Cosby, Bob Dylan, Margaret Mead, Marcel Marceau, and Carl Sagan have been among those taking the stage. Representing the last of the pre–rock-and-roll era for youth culture, the Crewcuts came to bring their barbershop brand of harmonies to Northern in a concert in Still Gym on April 2, 1956.

Beyond the music, arts, and culture town and gown share, there are less visible but nonetheless important services. Northern faculty and staff serve throughout the community in voluntary organizations, in providing expertise to business and local government, and in offering the community a library with two million volumes. Just one example of this sharing can be found in the work of retired communications professor Jim Lankford, who has studied hearing problems and hearing loss in those who work in agriculture. Many times in the summer, he would be found at rural festivals and county fairs offering testing and counsel to those whose hearing had been damaged by working with the machinery common on modern farms. In this image, farmers attending a farm show in 1997 wait for free testing.

The greatest benefit and the glue that holds town and gown together during times of tension is the role Northern plays in the local economy. The university is the largest employer in DeKalb County and has provided employment to tens of thousands of residents over the past century. The thousand-member faculty may be the most visible of Northern's workforce, but the two thousand civil service employees are the backbone of the university. These are the men and women, many of whom have deep family roots in DeKalb, who cook the meals, cut the grass, clean the buildings, and keep the telephones and computers running. They form the bridge that unites town and gown. As the university grew, so did the staff; the seventy-four kitchen workers of 1943 became the 381 kitchen workers of 1959. This picture dates to 1955.

castle on a hill

To keep the supplies coming to all areas of the university, Northern employs a small army of workers in materials management who deliver everything from paper clips to volatile gas canisters. Another group keeps the drivers' trucks running, and yet another, the grounds crew, keeps the sidewalks and drives plowed in the winter so deliveries can take place. In the photo above left, Jack Borders donned the stocking cap in the spirit of the Christmas season in 1979 while making his deliveries.

Town residents, too, contribute to the richness of town gown relations, perhaps none more than the Gliddens. The Glidden family has been at the center of local historical lore since the patriarch of the clan, Joseph, invented barbed wire in the old brick barn behind the Burger King on Lincoln Highway. A national historic marker on the grounds commemorates Joe's ingenuity. For over one hundred years, this family has continued to contribute its talent and resources to Northern.

Thousands of pedestrians and vehicles cross the intersection of Lucinda Avenue and Annie Glidden Road every day. Who were Annie and Lucinda that their names should mark such prominent DeKalb streets?

Annie, Joseph's niece, not only has the honor of having her name attached to one of the busiest roads in the county, she also has given her name to the small park just east of the Kishwaukee River at the Lucinda Bridge—Annie's Woods. The thousands traveling west on I-88 each day make her acquaintance at the Annie Glidden exit.

Early in the twentieth century, John Glidden built the house that, until recently, was home to the University Resources for Latinos on Annie Glidden Road across from Graham Hall. John sold the house to Annie when he moved his family to the old homestead on Lincoln Highway. Annie lived in what has more recently been called the Oderkirk House until she moved to Pasadena, California, in 1929.

According to local histories, Annie created some impressive gardens. She had studied agriculture at Cornell University, and her gardens and produce were the talk of all DeKalb. Set among the gardens at that time was the children's playhouse that now sits on the grounds of the Ellwood House. Annie's portrait is the centerpiece of a large mural depicting DeKalb history that greets all visitors to downtown DeKalb.

Annie Glidden, 1892

Lucinda Glidden

Eight years after his first wife died in childbirth in 1843, Annie's Uncle Joseph married Lucinda Warne in October of 1851. It is for her the city of DeKalb named Lucinda Avenue. In 1852, just one year after his marriage to Lucinda, DeKalb County voters elected Joe as their sheriff on the Democratic Party ticket. He was the last Democrat elected to countywide office in DeKalb County until 1978.

Lucinda and Joseph had just one child, Elva Frances, who was born in 1858. For fifteen years, Joseph Glidden worked his farm and dabbled in local politics, but with his invention of barbed wire in 1873, he became one of the most important people in the history of the county. Still, more alumni today likely know his wife's name, Lucinda, thanks to the avenue in her honor. Lucinda Avenue is the north border of the campus.

When DeKalb leaders sought to get the Illinois Legislature to put the new Northern Illinois Normal School here in the mid-1890s, Joseph Glidden not only lent his name and his connections to the campaign, he donated the land for the campus from his homestead farm. So it is only fitting that Annie Glidden Road and Lucinda Avenue are at the heart of Northern Illinois University's west campus.

Long life runs in the Glidden family: Joseph lived to be ninety-three, and Annie Glidden died in October 1965 at the age of one hundred. Long after the last family member is gone, there will still be the corner of Annie Glidden Road and Lucinda Avenue, one of the busiest in the city. The family's history is well documented in the extensive archives donated to Northern's Regional History Center by Joseph Glidden's grandnephew, Charles Bradt, who celebrated his one-hundred-first birthday in 2004.

A Northern Almanac

This section presents some new tables and lists that, taken together, comprise a Northern Almanac. Every effort has been made to verify the data and facts presented below, but it is inevitable there will be some disputes simply because of varying definitions of what constitutes an "official" school song, for example. This almanac will give all of Northern's friends and alumni both interesting information and a bit of fun as they poke into rather esoteric corners of campus and town history. Other resources that readers might tap if they do not find what they are looking for in the almanac are the University Archives, the Sports Information Department, and the Office of Institutional Research.

Sometimes it is difficult, if not impossible, to achieve an accuracy and consistency in statistics over a one-hundred-year time period. Precise records were not always kept, and, for example, official annual enrollment counts have been taken at various dates during the fall term over the years. Nonetheless, we have tried to be as accurate and consistent as possible where statistical data is presented. If you have particularly interesting facts to offer or historical materials to donate, we hope you will contact the University Archives to that end. And, of course, we are always eager to correct any errors you might find so long as you have irrefutable documentary evidence to support the correction.

NORTHERN MILESTONES

Northern history professor Earl W. Hayter included a list of important dates in his 1974 publication, *Education in Transition*. The chronology here begins where Hayter ended.

August 1, 1971	Richard J. Nelson appointed NIU's seventh president.
October 1, 1971	Center for Black Studies established.
January 2, 1977	Founders Memorial Library opened.
January 27, 1978	Richard Nelson resigned as president.
July 1978	NIU purchased first personal computer, a Commodore PET.
July 27, 1978	William R. Monat named NIU's eighth president.
September 21, 1978	Board of Regents established NIU Latino Studies Center.
August 31, 1979	Law College established.
May 22, 1980	Women's Studies minor established.
April 13, 1981	William the Goose killed.
August 1, 1982	Social Science Research Center established.

July 1, 1984	Board of Regents named William R. Monat first BOR chancellor.
January 24, 1985	Plant Molecular Biology Center established.
March 21, 1985	College of Engineering established.
March 22, 1985	Clyde Wingfield named NIU's ninth president.
August 1, 1985	Martin Luther King Jr. holiday established at NIU.
May 1986	John LaTourette named NIU's tenth president.
September 18, 1986	Center for Burma Studies established.
September 21, 1989	Faculty Senate established at NIU.
December 4, 1990	Hoffman Estates Center site approved.
August 30, 1995	NIU accessed the Internet.
August 1995	Rockford Center opened.
January 1, 1996	NIU Board of Trustees replaced the Board of Regents.
November 11, 1998	Naperville Center opened.
September 2000	Dennis and Stacey Barsema donated $24 million for College of Business building.
June 1, 2001	John Peters appointed NIU's eleventh president.
October 2004	Altgeld Hall reopened.
October 2005	Barsema Alumni Center opened.

SOME INTERESTING NIU FACTS...

Some significant, some trivial, some even disputed, but all interesting tidbits of information about Northern over the past century. With no overriding coherence or schema, these are arranged in the broad categories of the campus, athletics, student life, academics, and university administration. They offer good material for a Northern trivia contest.

The Northern Campus

First Campus Building: Altgeld Hall, officially the Administration Building until renaming in 1963. Designed by architect Charles Brush, construction took four years, and the building opened in September of 1899 to the first classes of students. Built at a cost of $230,160, Altgeld Hall featured a Tudor Gothic style favored by the man for whom it was named, John Peter Altgeld, governor of Illinois. Locals knew it as the Castle on a Hill, and its silhouette served as the Centennial logo.

First Women's Dormitory: Williston Hall opened in the fall of 1915 and was the third major building built on the campus. It bore President John Williston Cook's middle name since there was already a Cook Hall named for him at Illinois State University where he served as president before coming to Northern in 1899. Its popular name was Willy Hall; it housed 232 women and served as a dorm until 1969.

First Men's Dormitory: Gilbert Hall, with a capacity of 374 men, opened to its first residents in October of 1951. Named for Newell D. Gilbert, first DeKalb superintendent of schools, the building served as a dormitory until converted to administrative use in 1995.

First Campus Landmark: The Freshman Bench in the East Lagoon area dates to 1903 when it was a gift of that graduating class. The story associated with it is that a female student will remain a freshman until kissed by an upperclassman while sitting on the bench.

East Lagoon: It dates to the site visit by legislators in 1894 when locals diverted water from the Kishwaukee River to create a pond. A major WPA effort from 1934 to 1936 completely dredged the lagoon and created the landscaping we know today. It is approximately six acres in size, six feet deep at the north end, and nine feet deep toward the south end. The lagoon has been the site of many weddings, graduations, Springfests, classes, and concerts over the past century.

Lorusso Lagoon: Lorusso Lagoon is on the west end of campus and dates to the creation of Eco Park in the 1970s. Named for Anthony Lorusso, campus planning coordinator from 1950 to 1989, it is four feet deep in the center. Jia Wei Wang, the thirteen-year-old son of an NIU student, drowned in the lagoon July 20, 1990.

Kishwaukee River: One of the few rivers in North America that runs from south to north, the river's name comes from the Potawatomi word for cottonwood (or sycamore) tree. After a major flood in 1954, the U.S. Army Corps of Engineers rerouted parts of the river and built the levees along its banks that help to minimize flood damage today. The main branch is sixty-four miles long, and the drainage basin covers 786,100 acres.

Watson Crick: At the request of geneticist Sidney Mittler, Northern named the little creek that runs across the central campus after Nobel Prize winners James D. Watson and Francis H. Crick who developed the model for DNA molecular structure. Contractors completed a $6 million remake of the creek bed and the bridges and tunnels in July of 2003.

Biggest Single-Day Snowfall: Twenty inches of snow fell on January 13, 1979, as part of the Blizzard of '79 and one of the worst winters in history. This snow delayed the beginning of the spring semester a full week.

Biggest Single-Day Rainfall: Causing some of the most extensive flooding the campus has known, 8.03 inches of rain fell within a twenty-four-hour period July 17–18, 1996. This rain broke the record of 6.53 inches set in 1983. In third place is the 6.3 inches that fell on Dad's Day in October 1954 and also caused serious flooding.

Coldest Temperature Recorded: Twenty-seven degrees below zero recorded on January 20, 1985.

Hottest Temperature Recorded: One hundred six degrees recorded July 14, 1936. And there was, of course, no air conditioning. Highest dew point ever recorded occurred July 30, 1999, at 83; the heat index that day reached 115.

Tallest Building: The Holmes Student Center is 235 feet tall including the cupola on top that houses cooling, heating, and electrical equipment.

Veterans Flagpole: The NISTC Veterans Club erected the campus flagpole on June 2, 1956, as a memorial to all who have served their country in the armed services.

First Public Sculpture: As part of the festivities that inaugurated Rhoten Smith's tenure as Northern's sixth president, the university purchased Alexander Calder's steel stabile titled *Le Baron*. Calder created the sculpture in France and chose the campus site.

The Victory Bell: Service fraternity Alpha Phi Omega bought the bell in 1958 from a local school district and put it into a small shelter just east of Gabel Hall. It is to be rung after each Northern victory.

The Skating Bench: The large fieldstone skating bench just to the south of the lagoon came to Northern through a donation by the local Kiwanis Club, which also put in the fire ring.

Extended Campus: NIU currently owns land and facilities in four counties: Hoffman Estates and Naperville Centers in DuPage County, the main campus in DeKalb County, the Rockford Campus in Winnebago County, and the Lorado Taft Campus in Ogle County.

King Commons: At the very center of the campus, Martin Luther King Jr. Commons serves as a free speech and gathering space with two public sculptures, sculptor Peter Fagan's bust of King and artist Dan Nardi's towering *Balance of Equality*.

Montgomery Arboretum: One of two preserved wooded areas on the campus, the arboretum was part of the original deed of land for a campus from Joseph Glidden. Through the years, it has hosted many classes, various protests, and a whistle stop speech by presidential candidate Teddy Roosevelt.

Annie Glidden Road: The main road cutting through the west end of the campus is named for Joseph Glidden's niece, Annie. There is also a public park called Annie's Woods along the Kishwaukee River at the east edge of the campus.

Northern Athletics

First Athletic Coach: Fred Lemar Charles, biology professor, doubled as Northern's first coach of intercollegiate athletics when he organized the baseball team in the spring of 1900. Charles also coached the first women's intercollegiate basketball team in 1900. John L. Keith, a student, coached the first football team in the fall of 1899 and the men's basketball team of 1899.

First Olympic Athlete: Le Roy Davison, a middleweight boxer, earned a place on the 1940 U.S. Olympic Team. Unfortunately, World War II cancelled the 1940 and 1944 Olympics. Davison flew bombing runs into Germany early in the war and then was shot down and wounded in the South Pacific in 1943. He survived alone in the jungle for over a month and returned home a war hero.

Olympic Gold Medalist: Ken Henry, a Northern student, won a Gold Medal in the 500-meter speed skating event in Oslo, Norway, in 1952. He is the only Northern student ever to win Olympic gold.

First All-American Female Athlete: Janet Wentworth, a native of Penticton, British Columbia, placed third in the nation in the badminton championships of 1980.

First All-American Male Athlete: Bill Terwilliger won the AAU decathlon title in 1942 following his graduation from NIU and was an AAU All-American. In more conventional terms, Floyd Hunsberger made Honorable Mention AP All-America in football in 1948.

First National Championship: The men's cross-country team won the national title over a four-mile course in Chicago in November 1958.

First Women's Basketball Game: The Glidden Society defeated the Ellwood Society 6 to 5, March 8, 1900.

First Men's Basketball Game: The Gliddens defeated the Ellwoods 21 to 11 in February 1900.

First Football Game: Northern defeated DeKalb High School 16 to 10, November 10, 1899.

First Athletic Financial Aid: The Booster Club raised funds to support worthy students and made the first award in 1955. The awards were to cover about half of school costs and averaged $405.

First Women's Athletic Financial Aid: In 1977, Northern awarded twenty-three athletic stipends across eleven women's sports.

First Female Head Coach: Northern hired Jessica Foster as Director of Physical Training in 1901, and she coached the basketball team, replacing Fred Charles.

First African American Head Coach: Willie Kimmons coached cross-country from 1970 to 1973. Emory Luck became Northern's first minority head coach in a major sport when he took over the men's basketball program May 28, 1973.

First African American Female Head Coach: Northern hired Liz McQuitter Galloway to coach women's basketball on July 1, 1994.

First African American Athlete: Elzie Cooper from Rochelle played three sports for Northern from 1933 to 1936: football, basketball, and baseball.

First Football Broadcast: On November 11, 1939, WMRO in Aurora broadcast a football game in which Illinois State Normal defeated Northern 13 to 7.

Glidden Field: Situated along the banks of the mighty Kishwaukee, Glidden Field served as home for the football team for sixty-six years.

Huskie Stadium: Although in use for the 1965 season and dedicated November 11, 1965, the stadium was not officially named until April of 1974 during the university's celebration of its seventy-fifth anniversary.

Anderson Hall: Named for longtime women's physical education professor Miriam Anderson, Anderson Hall was the original home of virtually all of women's intercollegiate sports at Northern.

Gymnasia: The first was in Altgeld Hall on the main floor below grade; the second built was Still Gym (1928); then gymnasia followed in Gabel (1958) and Anderson (1964) Halls. Evans Field House (1957) was the primary site for intercollegiate contests until the NIU Convocation Center opened in October 2002. There are also gyms for intramural use in the Recreation Center and Huskie Stadium.

Student Life

Campus Mascots: Besides the traditional Victor E. Huskie, the campus has had two animal mascots of note: Betsy the Bear and William the Goose. Betsy came to Northern's zoo as a small black bear cub, a gift from Perry Ellwood. She died December 20, 1907, was stuffed, and then mounted inside Altgeld Hall. William resided near the lagoon and attracted national attention in 1976 when administrators tried to move him out. A student under the influence of marijuana killed him April 13, 1981.

First Year Enrollment: One hundred seventy-three students enrolled in the fall of 1899, one hundred forty-six women and twenty-seven men. Almost half were between the ages of twenty-one and forty.

First International Student: Six students from the Philippines arrived at Northern in the fall of 1904: Antonio Nera, Joseph Cabrera, Gregorio Manuel, Segundo Hipolito, Mariano Carbonell, and Gregorio Ramirez.

First Edition of the Student Newspaper: The *Northern Illinois* first edition came out in October of 1899 as a monthly paper, fourteen pages long. All but three students subscribed to the paper, generating the revenue needed to publish.

First Alumni Newspaper: Alumni Recall published May 5, 1926.

First Homecoming: In October of 1903, a group of alumni played Northern in a football game; the term *homecoming* did not appear until October of 1906.

First Winter Carnival: January 19–20, 1945.

First African American Graduate: Fanny Ruth Patterson from Hinckley, Illinois, graduated in 1915.

Black History Month: Began as Afro-American History Week on Sunday, February 9, 1969. James Farmer, nationally known civil rights leader and former director of CORE, began the week with a speech in the Sandburg Auditorium.

Springfest: Springfest at Northern began as May Day Dance on May 1, 1900. May Day Dance became May Fete in 1918 and continued until the name changed to Springfest in 1974.

Band Uniforms: Northern debuted band uniforms in red, white, and black in the 1932 Homecoming parade.

First Edition of **Towers***:* Sigma Tau Delta and Nu Iota Pi first published Northern's undergraduate literary journal as a supplement to the student newspaper January 31, 1939.

First Civil Rights Protest: A student rally on November 21, 1946, began a boycott of the Log Cabin Restaurant in DeKalb for its refusal to serve Ernest C. Smith, an African American war veteran. The boycott was successful.

Railroad Track Fatalities: Local newspapers have recorded the deaths of nine students on the Chicago North Western tracks, which run through DeKalb just south of the campus, over the past twenty years: Beth Ann Davis, Mike Prater, Paul Avon, Katrina Tabor, Jamie Tucker, Jay Mears, Robert Morgan, Glenn J. Christiansen, and Kenneth McInnis.

World War I Casualties: Northern's enrollment in 1917 included 424 women and 58 men; in the fall of 1918, 223 women and no men. Four men who had been at Northern died in World War I: Howard Byers, Wendell Lindberg, Clinton Glidden, and Martin Chase.

World War II Casualties: A total of thirty-seven Northern students lost their lives in World War II, the first being Marsh Hemenway, killed on duty off Florida, February 15, 1942. The first to die in combat was Harold Lewis in the North Africa Campaign, December 5, 1942.

Accidental Deaths: A total of ninety-three students are known to have died from accidents while enrolled at Northern, most in automobile crashes. One of the most unusual deaths happened to a student walking home from the downtown bars. He had stashed an empty beer glass in his side pocket before leaving the bar. Near the DeKalb Public Library, he slipped and fell on the empty beer glass that shattered, slashing the artery in his thigh. He died within minutes on the sidewalk. In a strikingly similar accident, a female student died when a beer glass thrown in a downtown bar broke and slashed the artery in her neck. She, too, died within minutes of being cut.

First School Songs: Music professor A. Neil Annas wrote the first official school song, titled "Alma Mater," in 1913. Annas wrote two other songs that were also popular in subsequent years, "Castle on the Hill" and "Loyalty Song" (1925–1930). They, too, served as school songs for a time.

First School Colors: Northern's official school colors, by vote of the students on October 15, 1899, are yellow and white. The Athletic Association adopted colors of black and red in 1907. Celebrations using yellow and white continued as late as the 1930s, and those are still the official school colors. In recent decades, only the athletic colors of cardinal and black have been used.

Tuition, 1899: None. Northern advertised itself as Tuition Free—and it was.

First Sorority: Sigma Chi Sigma came to Northern in 1931 as a local sorority and then affiliated with Sigma Sigma Sigma in 1944. The first national social sorority on Northern's campus was Delta Sigma Epsilon, which established the Alpha Omicron chapter with thirty-five pledges April 29, 1944. This chapter merged into Delta Zeta in 1956. A week earlier, on April 22, 1944, fourteen pledges were informally initiated into the Gamma chapter of Delta Kappa Chi, which had state affiliation.

First Fraternity: Alpha Phi Omega organized as a service fraternity in 1928. A local fraternity, Alpha Delta Chi, petitioned to Phi Sigma Epsilon and was installed on May 19, 1947, to become the first social fraternity on the Northern campus. The Student Association approved a constitution for this chapter April 22, 1947.

Academic Affairs

First Day of Classes: Tuesday, September 12, 1899.

First Class Taught at Northern: President John Williston Cook taught the first class, psychology, to seniors in the first hour of the day that first semester.

First Two-Year Degree: Sixteen students graduated in June 1900, and since they received degrees in alphabetical order, the first graduate was Jennie Bertram from Idaho Falls, Idaho.

First Bachelor's Degree: In June of 1911, James Richard Grant earned the first full four-year bachelor's degree from Northern. Grant was from Dover, Arkansas.

First Master's Degree: President Leslie Holmes conferred the first master's degree (English) on Constance Chenette Bax from DeKalb, June 1, 1952.

First Doctoral Degree: Herbert J. Bergstein received the EdD in business education, June 6, 1964.

First Scholarship Funds: The Northern Illinois Teachers Association established a loan fund of $300 in 1900. Mrs. Fred Charles donated the first memorial fund, $300 for loans, in memory of her husband, Professor Fred L. Charles. The first estate bequeathed to Northern came from a local farmer, Andrew Brown, and totaled about $22,000 when President Cook sold the land and buildings in 1919.

First Endowed Chair: Although Northern enjoyed corporate support for several positions in the 1980s, that support was partial and not permanent. The first endowed chair came to the College of Education in June of 1995 with a gift of $1.7 million from John P. and Ruth Morgridge in honor of 1915 Northern graduates Ruth Gordon Morgridge and L D Morgridge.

First Library: Northern's first library was the Haish Library set on the second floor of Altgeld Hall. Ella Warwick was the librarian and Grace L. Babbitt, her assistant. The Haish Library served for a half-century until the Swen Parson Library opened in 1952.

First Privately Funded Building: Dennis and Stacey Barsema donated $24 million in stock for the construction of Barsema Hall, the home of the College of Business, in September of 2000.

First Library Book: *Legends of the Virgin and Christ* by H. A. Guerber, published in 1897. Purchased November 15, 1899, the book cost $.94.

R.O.T.C. Program: The program came to NIU through a formal vote of the University Council, after much debate on the campus, during the peak of the Vietnam War. In a special meeting February 21, 1968, the Council voted 17 aye, 7 nay, and 4 abstentions.

NIU's First Personal Computer: The university purchased a Commodore PET computer in July of 1978 for $810; it boasted 4K RAM, a cassette tape drive, and an eight-inch monochrome monitor.

Library's First Personal Computer: A Timex Sinclair purchased at Kmart, June 20, 1983, for $64.95. It had a cassette tape drive and 4K RAM.

First Mainframe Computer: Northern acquired an IBM 1620 through a lease-purchase in June 1964.

First Honorary Society on Campus: Alpha Psi Omega, dramatic arts honorary, came to Northern in June 1931; the local chapter deactivated in the fall of 1967.

M&M Peanuts Inventor: NIU marketing professor John McNamara invented the M&M Peanut candies during his tenure as president of M&M Division of Mars Candies (1945–1959). McNamara earned his BEd at Northern in 1931 and forged a career in business while still continuing his education until he completed a doctorate at Purdue. Later in his life, he taught at NIU for seven years and authored a marketing textbook before retiring in 1978.

Organization of the Colleges: Following the change to university status in 1957, a faculty committee recommended the change from academic divisions to the colleges commonly found in American universities. The first colleges began operations in the summer of 1959: Education, Liberal Arts and Sciences, and Fine and Applied Arts.

Faculty Club: Organized December 14, 1918, the Faculty Club was the oldest continuous faculty organization on campus. Though it never enjoyed a building to provide services to the faculty, the club provided social activities and retirement recognition for faculty for eighty years. The Faculty Club disbanded in 1998.

Extension Classes: Faculty first offered formal classes off-campus in 1939 with a faculty member serving as a part-time director of extension classes.

NIU by the Numbers at Age 100: As Northern completed its first century, it had seven degree-granting colleges comprised of forty-one academic departments. Northern offered twenty-one different degrees with fifty-one undergraduate majors and fifty-seven minor fields of study. Graduates pursued degrees in seventy majors.

Administration and Staff

Employees: Northern employs just fewer than 4,000 people as faculty (1,000), civil service staff (2,100), and supportive professional staff (800). NIU also employs approximately 1,000 graduate assistants and thousands of students part-time.

First Staff Employees: Librarian Elma Warwick and her assistant, Grace Babbitt, 1899.

The Presidents: There have been eleven presidents:

John Williston Cook	1899–1919
J. Stanley Brown	1919–1927
J. Clifton Brown	1927–1929
Karl L. Adams	1929–1948
Leslie A. Holmes	1949–1967
Rhoten A. Smith	1967–1971
Richard J. Nelson	1971–1978
William R. Monat	1978–1985
Clyde Wingfield	1985–1986
John E. LaTourette	1986–2000
John Peters	2000–

Cook had the longest tenure in office of twenty years and one month.

Vice President and Provost, Academic Affairs: First held by J. Robert Hainds, this position evolved from Academic Vice President (1961–1963) to Executive Vice President and Provost (1963–1968) with Francis Geigle, and then became Vice President Academic Affairs and Provost with Richard C. Bowers's appointment in 1968.

Vice President, Business Affairs: Z. Harold Dorland became Northern's first in 1965.

Vice President, Administrative Affairs: Created by President William Monat in 1985, Eddie R. Williams has been the only person to hold this position at NIU.

First Vice President, Minority: Eddie R. Williams, Administrative Affairs, 1985.

First Dean, Minority: Professor Alfonso Thurman, College of Education, 1996.

First Dean, Female: Barbara Seelye, College of Professional Studies, 1974–1980.

First Vice President, Female: Margaret Barr, Vice President of Student Affairs, 1982–1985.

Altgeld Hall Administrative Offices: The President's Office returned to Altgeld in the fall of 2004 along with many other administrative offices. The $29 million for rehabilitation is 126 times the cost of the original construction ($230,120).

First Superintendent of Physical Plant: George Shoop headed the staff at Altgeld Hall from 1899 till 1915. When it first opened, Altgeld Hall even had its own electric generator that supplied power for the lighting, and Shoop kept the generator and boilers running in addition to overseeing two janitors who did the cleaning and repairs. And this he did dressed in a suit, white shirt, and tie.

Salary Inflation: John W. Cook came to Northern in 1899 at a salary of $5,000 per year and left at the same salary in 1919. Using Consumer Price Index data from the Federal Reserve Bank, that salary would equal $92,950 in 2003. President Peters's salary in 2003 was almost three times that at $265,000. Cook's responsibilities, however, included only one building, two dozen faculty and staff, and several hundred students; today, Northern has almost 4,000 faculty and staff, 24,000 students, and campuses in four counties. The average faculty salary in 1900 was $1,500 per year; faculty salaries have grown at twice the rate of the CPI over the intervening century though the responsibilities and workload changed little.

Average Number of Photos Shot Each Year in the 1990s by Imaging Services: 35,000. In January of 2003, Imaging Services switched from traditional negative exposure and print photography to digital imaging.

Projecting Continued Growth: If Northern's enrollment were to grow over the next one hundred years as it did from 1899 to 1999, the enrollment in 2099 would be 3,240,000. These students would be taught by 62,500 faculty on sixteen campuses scattered throughout the region.

Branch Campuses

Northern Illinois University owns land in four counties and maintains branch campuses in Oregon, Rockford, Hoffman Estates, and Naperville. The university holds several hundred acres of prairie preserve in Ogle County.

Lorado Taft
Northern acquired the Lorado Taft campus at Oregon through a legislative act signed into law by Governor Adlai Stevenson, August 7, 1951. Chicago sculptor Lorado Taft used this land, sixty-six acres adjacent to Lowden State Park, as a summer residence for himself and colleagues and called it Eagle's Nest. Among the sculptures still extant on the grounds, none is known so well as the towering Blackhawk statue that rises majestically above the trees over the Rock River. This field campus serves as the home to NIU's Outdoor Education Program and offers a place for thousands of Illinois schoolchildren to get out of their classrooms and into the woods for botanical exploration.

Rockford Education Center
Through legislative act, Northern broke ground for a center in Rockford in June 1994 on ten acres of land on the southeast corner of the city at the junction of U.S. 20 and I-90. The $6 million center opened for classes in August of 1995 and offers fifteen classrooms, a computer lab, an auditorium, conference rooms, a library, and administrative office space. Classes previously offered at various sites throughout Rockford are now offered in one place with excellent access and facilities. The Rockford Center offers 40,000 square feet of space for NIU programs to reach its Winnebago County constituency.

Hoffman Estates Education Center

The Village of Hoffman Estates donated the 3.9 acres of land that it had been given by Sears to the university to build a facility adjacent to the new Sears headquarters. Located near the junction of I-90 and Illinois 59, this site has excellent access and has consolidated programs and courses previously offered at various western suburban venues. Designed by Homart Development, this center offers 46,000 square feet, including sixteen classrooms, computer labs, conference spaces, an auditorium, a library, and administrative offices. NIU broke ground for this facility October 10, 1991, and celebrated its Grand Opening, October 29, 1992.

Naperville Center

Built at a cost of $20 million, the Naperville Center facility offers 113,000 square feet, including twelve classrooms, two computer labs, and a large multipurpose area that hosts small conferences and similar events. The center is the home for NIU Business and Industry Services and the North Central Education Laboratory, which assists in continuing education for teachers. The emphasis is on teaching and public service tailored to the surrounding communities. Business, engineering, and education classes are offered for those who are employed full-time but want to continue their education. NIU planners chose the site for its easy access to both mass transit and major highways for those attending evening and weekend classes.

OF SEALS, SONGS, CHEERS, AND MASCOTS

Official Seals (seals shown on following pages)

Northern has adopted a number of official seals over the past one hundred years to reflect changes in name and status.

When the Legislature granted increased status with a name change to Northern Illinois State Teachers College in July 1921, a new seal followed. Trustees dropped the "Teachers" from the name in 1955, and the official seal then reflected the new Northern name.

The Illinois Legislature conferred university status on Northern beginning July 1, 1957, and that brought another change in the official seal. The new university seal would last nearly forty years until the Centennial Celebration brought yet another iteration.

The fifth and final seal of Northern's first century came in 1995 as part of the Centennial Celebration and featured the Castle on a Hill from which the university had grown.

Earliest Seal

Fifth and Final Seal

School Colors, Songs, and Cheers

To the surprise of many, Northern's official school colors are yellow and white. They have been for one hundred years. The first edition of the student newspaper reported: "At the morning exercises Wednesday, October 15 [1899], Miss Stratford, as chairman, reported Yellow and White as the choice of the committee on colors for the NISNS." After a general discussion, these colors were adopted. All of the earliest pennants and banners reflect this choice, as does the first school song, "The Yellow and the White." In January of 1901, the *Northern Illinois* first published this song in three verses that began with the lines: "Sing to the colors that float in the sky, Hurrah for the yellow and the white!" The song ends with these two lines: "Hail! Hail to the Normal whose colors we wear, Hurrah for the yellow and the white!"

With the beginnings of the Northern Illinois Athletic Association came pressure to adopt athletic colors more appropriate to the football gridiron and the basketball court. The NIAA in December of 1906 decided on a monogram for the Northern sports teams and chose red and black as the school's athletic colors. Nonetheless, no official action by the students, the faculty, or the administration ever disestablished the yellow and the white nor officially adopted the red and the black. Athletic pennants from the 1920s and 1930s continued to be made in yellow and white. In 1934, the student newspaper encouraged everyone to participate in Homecoming: "Let's all wear yellow chrysanthemums at the football game! What difference does it make if you are fellows? Maybe you can get paper ones somewhere." By the 1940s, the red and the black had virtually driven any memory of the yellow and the white into the archives trivia file, and today, Northern's colors are known to all as red and black.

Students sang many songs at social gatherings and athletic contests early in Northern's history, and there was no official single alma mater or fight song as we know them today. The first known school song was sung to the tune of the "Orange and Black" and published in the October 1906 edition of the *Northern Illinois*:

> In rally game or contest,
> Where victory's won by might,
> We'll stand by our own colors
> The yellow and the white.
> Then on we'll cheer our comrades,
> And raise our banners high,
> While the Northern Normal conquers,
> With its motto strong, "Stand By."

Music professor A. Neil Annas wrote the classics that served for Northern's first half-century: "Castle on the Hill," "Alma Mater," and "Loyalty Song." Over the past one hundred years, many popular songs were adapted for Northern's use by writing local lyrics to popular tunes and then printing these into pocket-sized songbooks. Most of the songs in these books are not attributed to any author. Two institutional name changes in the mid-1950s (NISTC to NISC to NIU) brought a rewriting of Annas's "Loyalty Song" and the writing of a new "Alma Mater Hymn," which first appears in archival documentation in 1960, unattributed. The "Huskie Fight Song" first appears—also unattributed—in the May 8, 1963, issue of the *Northern Star*. There is archival documentation proving authorship: a signed letter from physical education professor Francis Stroup dated October 31, 1961, proposes the lyrics that were adopted. The fight song music is a modest rewrite of the chorus to Annas's "Loyalty Song." The NIU fight song has remained virtually unchanged now for thirty years. The lyrics of the "Alma Mater" have changed since it first appeared (sixteen of the forty-three words changed). The fight song has been used regularly at athletic events, the alma mater rarely.

Huskie Fight Song

Huskies! Come on you Huskies!
And make a score or two,
Huskies, you're Northern Huskies—
The team to pull us through.
Forward, together, forward!
There's a victory in view,
Come on you Huskies,
Fight on you Huskies,
And win for N.I.U.!

Two choruses of the fight song are normally followed by the cheer:
H - U - S - K - I - E - S   Go, Huskies!

Mascot

From its founding, the Northern sports teams have been known as the Huskies, and the yellow and white pennants from the early twentieth century featured the profile of a huskie. For a number of years in the 1930s, local sportswriters referred to Northern teams as the "Profs," but that name was neither official nor long-lived. An actual huskie dog has never been traditional at Northern, but in recent decades, Victor E. Huskie—a student in "uniform"—has attended many sporting and public relations events.

On-Campus Fall Enrollment

Undergraduate Figures, 1899–1950

1899	173	1912	401	1925	692	1938	951
1900	217	1913	441	1926	557	1939	1,165
1901	220	1914	455	1927	514	1940	1,173
1902	234	1915	466	1928	654	1941	1,008
1903	218	1916	482	1929	701	1942	803
1904	220	1917	334	1930	760	1943	441
1905	261	1918	334	1931	729	1944	498
1906	297	1919	256	1932	837	1945	581
1907	303	1920	335	1933	792	1946	1,442
1908	318	1921	402	1934	743	1947	1,635
1909	316	1922	516	1935	715	1948	1,668
1910	359	1923	533	1936	768	1949	2,073
1911	366	1924	631	1937	769	1950	1,986

Undergraduate and Graduate Figures, 1951–2003

	Ugr.	Gr.	Total		Ugr.	Gr.	Law	Total
1951	1,705	188	1,893	1974	15,540	4,562		20,102
1952	1,780	220	2,000	1975	15,953	5,316		21,269
1953	2,040	245	2,285	1976	16,595	5,095		21,690
1954	2,313	256	2,569	1977	16,607	4,663		21,270
1955	2,899	361	3,260	1978	17,079	4,590		21,669
1956	3,674	451	4,125	1979	17,411	4,370	349	22,130
1957	4,278	466	4,744	1980	17,848	4,350	308	22,506
1958	4,940	717	5,657	1981	18,068	4,195	251	22,514
1959	5,125	987	6,112	1982	18,394	3,897	267	22,558
1960	5,747	1,295	7,042	1983	17,650	3,742	257	21,649
1961	6,458	1,653	8,111	1984	17,322	3,636	271	21,229
1962	7,347	1,790	9,137	1985	17,908	3,875	244	22,027
1963	8,724	1,913	10,637	1986	18,106	3,929	245	22,280
1964	10,326	2,346	12,672	1987	18,649	4,192	277	23,118
1965	11,950	2,738	14,688	1988	17,878	4,288	297	22,463
1966	13,095	3,345	16,440	1989	17,813	4,367	316	22,496
1967	14,440	3,617	18,057	1990	18,027	4,344	308	22,679
1968	16,370	4,349	20,719	1991	18,015	4,427	297	22,739
1969	17,610	4,909	22,519	1992	17,240	4,482	290	22,012
1970	17,581	5,236	22,817	1993	16,609	4,539	310	21,458
1971	17,962	4,857	22,819	1994	16,536	4,356	329	21,221
1972	16,702	4,368	21,070	1995	15,607	4,230	300	20,137
1973	15,465	4,506	19,971	1996	15,227	4,039	294	19,560

1997	15,665	4,028	280	19,993
1998	16,182	3,844	282	20,308
1999	16,751	3,744	276	20,801
2000	16,991	3,640	297	20,928
2001	17,304	3,883	303	21,490
2002	17,887	4,026	331	22,244
2003	18,011	4,144	334	22,489

DEKALB POTPOURRI

Origins: The State Legislature created DeKalb County March 4, 1837, by splitting Kane County in two. The first white settlers came in 1835, John B. Codins and Norman C. Moore. Traditional town founder Russell Huntley arrived in February 1837.

Names: DeKalb was first known as Huntley's Grove (1837–1847), then Buena Vista (1847–1849), before becoming DeKalb Center in 1849. Local officials shortened the name to DeKalb in 1883.

Namesake: Baron Johann von DeKalb was a Hessian mercenary in the American Revolutionary War. DeKalb attained the rank of major general in Washington's army; he was wounded, taken prisoner, and died in August of 1780.

Population: The population of DeKalb in 1890 was 2,579; in 1990, 34,925; in 2000, 39,018.

Founder: Among DeKalb's first settlers was Russell Huntley, who established a log cabin "hotel" in 1838; the first post office opened inside this hotel February 8, 1849.

Barbed Wire: The DeKalb "patriarchs" who brought Northern to DeKalb were Isaac Ellwood, Jacob Haish, and Joseph Glidden. Glidden invented barbed wire in 1873, and both Haish and Ellwood made fortunes manufacturing barbed wire. All were instrumental in the founding of Northern in the 1890s.

Newspaper: The fourth party honored as a founder of Northern was Clinton Rosette, the editor of the *DeKalb Chronicle* (1879–1909), who was also a political activist. The *Chronicle* remains today as DeKalb's only daily newspaper.

"The Ag": Hybrid seed corn came to world use through a branch of the DeKalb Farm Bureau founded in 1919 as the Pure Seed Association. It is today DeKalb AgResearch, a part of the Monsanto Company, and has one of the best-known trademarks in agriculture, the Winged Ear.

Wurlitzer: The Wurlitzer Company had its headquarters in DeKalb from 1919 to 1981 and manufactured pianos, organs, and jukeboxes sold around the world.

Mass Media: DeKalb has three newspapers and five radio stations, including one paper and two radio stations courtesy of NIU.

Farming: The DeKalb County Farm Bureau is tied for the oldest in the country with the Kendall County Farm Bureau and dates to June 1, 1912.

First Church: The Baptists claim the first formal congregation and date their presence to 1842.

Mass Transit: The Huskie Line serves as basic public mass transit in DeKalb and is the second largest bus system in the state in terms of passengers carried, 2.7 million each year.

Governance: Political governance includes seats for students on the city council, a part-time elected mayor, and a full-time city manager.

VIP: DeKalb's most famous daughter is Cindy Crawford, once internationally known as a fashion model, MTV hostess, and film actress.

VIP: Willard Wirtz, secretary of labor in the Kennedy administration, was the son of a faculty member. Wirtz Hall bears the family name.

VIPs: Brothers George and Henry Gurler brought important advancements to dairy farming late in the nineteenth century and earned national renown. Their town home is still preserved, just a block east of the Ellwood House.

VIP: Tom Roberts Sr. came to DeKalb as an ag extension agent in the 1920s and eventually founded DeKalb AgResearch Incorporated.

VIPs—The "Patriarchs": The three men instrumental in the invention of barbed wire and its manufacture in DeKalb: Joseph Glidden, Jacob Haish, and Isaac Ellwood.

Nicknames: DeKalb High School sports teams are known as the Barbs in honor of the invention of barbed wire in DeKalb. The school paper is the *Barblet*, and the mascot is Barbie Crow. DeKalb is still sometimes called "The Barb City."

The River: The Kishwaukee River is one of only a few rivers in North America that flows south to north into the Rock River. Kishwaukee is a Potawatomi word meaning "cottonwood tree."

The Railroad: The Galena and Chicago Union Railroad first came to DeKalb on August 12, 1853. One hundred fifty years later, over forty trains a day pass through downtown.

Monuments: There are three monuments to war veterans: the Army tank at First and Lincoln, the clock at First and Lincoln, and the large statue on the courthouse lawn in Sycamore honoring those who served in the Civil War.

Location: DeKalb is fifty-eight miles west of the Chicago Loop via I-88, the Ronald Reagan Tollway.

Altitude: DeKalb's altitude is 886 feet above sea level.

Libraries: The DeKalb Public Library began on the second floor of City Hall, July 1, 1893. Through his estate, Jacob Haish provided for the current facility, and it is named in his honor, as was Northern's first library (which also received Haish funding).

Fire Department: The Fire Department began as a hook and ladder volunteer company in 1869; the first paid fireman came on duty February 4, 1904. DeKalb has provided fire services to the university through a contract for a century.

Police Department: The DeKalb Police Department dates to July 22, 1885; prior to that, the county sheriff and the justice of the peace kept order.

First Murder: DeKalb did not record a murder until 1854 when a local Irish laborer suffered a broken neck when hit over the head with a chair.

Soils: DeKalb County farmland is among the richest in the world, having long been natural prairie growing in the soils deposited by the retreat of the last glaciers.

Average Annual Rainfall: 36.74 inches.

Average Annual Snowfall: 33.2 inches.

INDEX

INDEX

INDEX

INDEX

INDEX

ABOUT THE AUTHOR

Glen A. Gildemeister is director of the Regional History Center at Northern Illinois University and the university archivist.